Acting Edition

Off Off Broadway Festival Plays, 49th Series

Beethoven's Third
by Howard Ho

Data Queen
by Adam Ashraf Elsayigh

A Definitive Ranking of My Closest Friends
by Jay Stalder

A Mercy at Midnight Castle
by Phillip Gregory Burke

A Neo-Vagina Monologue
by Aster Aguilar

Pilloried
by Jillian Blevins

SAMUEL FRENCH

Beethoven's Third © 2025 by Howard Ho
Data Queen © 2025 by Adam Ashraf Elsayigh
A Definitive Ranking of My Closest Friends © 2025 by Jay Stalder
A Mercy at Midnight Castle © 2025 by Phillip Gregory Burke
A Neo-Vagina Monologue © 2025 by Aster Aguilar
Pilloried © 2025 by Jillian Blevins
All Rights Reserved

OFF OFF BROADWAY FESTIVAL PLAYS, 49TH SERIES is fully protected under the copyright laws of the United States of America, the British Commonwealth, including Canada, and all member countries of the Berne Convention for the Protection of Literary and Artistic Works, the Universal Copyright Convention, and/or the World Trade Organization conforming to the Agreement on Trade Related Aspects of Intellectual Property Rights. All rights, including professional and amateur stage productions, recitation, lecturing, public reading, motion picture, radio broadcasting, television, online/digital production, and the rights of translation into foreign languages are strictly reserved.

ISBN 978-0-573-71161-9

www.concordtheatricals.com
www.concordtheatricals.co.uk

FOR PRODUCTION INQUIRIES

UNITED STATES AND CANADA
info@concordtheatricals.com
1-866-979-0447

UNITED KINGDOM AND EUROPE
licensing@concordtheatricals.co.uk
020-7054-7298

Each title is subject to availability from Concord Theatricals Corp., depending upon country of performance. Please be aware that *OFF OFF BROADWAY FESTIVAL PLAYS, 49TH SERIES* may not be licensed by Concord Theatricals Corp. in your territory. Professional and amateur producers should contact the nearest Concord Theatricals Corp. office or licensing partner to verify availability.

CAUTION: Professional and amateur producers are hereby warned that *OFF OFF BROADWAY FESTIVAL PLAYS, 49TH SERIES* is subject to a licensing fee. The purchase, renting, lending or use of this book does not constitute a license to perform this title(s), which license must be obtained from Concord Theatricals Corp. prior to any performance. Performance of this title(s) without a license is a violation of federal law and may subject the producer and/or presenter of such performances to civil penalties. Both amateurs and professionals considering a production are strongly advised to apply to the appropriate agent before starting rehearsals, advertising, or booking a theatre. A licensing fee must be paid whether the title(s) is presented for charity or gain and whether or not admission is charged. Professional/Stock licensing fees are quoted upon application to Concord Theatricals Corp.

This work is published by Samuel French, an imprint of Concord Theatricals Corp.

No one shall make any changes in this title(s) for the purpose of production. No part of this book may be reproduced, stored in a retrieval system, scanned, uploaded, or transmitted in any form, by any means, now known or yet to be invented, including mechanical, electronic, digital, photocopying, recording, videotaping, or otherwise, without the prior written permission of the publisher. No one shall share this title(s), or any part of this title(s), through any social media or file hosting websites.

For all inquiries regarding motion picture, television, online/digital and other media rights, please contact Concord Theatricals Corp.

MUSIC AND THIRD-PARTY MATERIALS USE NOTE

Licensees are solely responsible for obtaining formal written permission from copyright owners to use copyrighted music and/or other copyrighted third-party materials (e.g. artworks, logos) in the performance of this play and are strongly cautioned to do so. If no such permission is obtained by the licensee, then the licensee must use only original music and materials that the licensee owns and controls. Licensees are solely responsible and liable for clearances of all third-party copyrighted materials, including without limitation music, and shall indemnify the copyright owners of the play(s) and their licensing agent, Concord Theatricals Corp., against any costs, expenses, losses and liabilities arising from the use of such copyrighted third-party materials by licensees. For music, please contact the appropriate music licensing authority in your territory for the rights to any incidental music.

IMPORTANT BILLING AND CREDIT REQUIREMENTS

If you have obtained performance rights to this title, please refer to your licensing agreement for important billing and credit requirements.

Concord Theatricals presents The Samuel French Off Off Broadway Short Play Festival (OOB) has been the nation's leading short play festival for forty-nine years. The OOB Festival has served as a doorway to future success for aspiring writers. Over two hundred plays have been published, and many participants have become established, award-winning playwrights.

For more information on the Off Off Broadway Short Play Festival, including history, interviews, and more, please visit www.oobfestival.com.

2024 HONORARY GUEST PLAYWRIGHT
Jen Silverman

2024 FESTIVAL JUDGES
Nathan Alan Davis
Emmanuel Wilson
Margaret Ledford
Jiehae Park
Madhuri Shekar
Cezar Williams
Liza Birkenmeier
Julia Izumi
Alexis Williams
Theresa Rebeck
Michael Walkup
Nan Barnett

Festival Sponsor: Concord Theatricals

Festival Co-Artistic Directors: Casey McLain, Garrett Anderson

Client Liaison: Abbie Van Nostrand

House Manager: Tyler Mullen

Box Office Manager: Rosemary Bucher

Marketing Team: Meredith Foster, Jeremiah Hernandez, Courtney Kochuba, and Imogen Lloyd Webber

Festival Production Coordinator: Katie Priscott

Festival Support Staff: Shaina Gilks, Kristen Rea, Rachel Smith, Elizabeth Minski, Victoria Bond, Natty Koper, Ranana Chernin, Gabriela Morales, Nate Netzley, Ella Andrew, Jeremiah Hernandez, Max Bahneman, Meredith Foster

2024 Submission Readers: Amy Rose Marsh, Rachel Levens, Kristen Rea, Debbie McLean, Faith Williams, Elizabeth Minski, Stephanie Cerino, Jackson Used, Alexander Perez, Meredith Foster, Ben Keiper, Abbie Van Nostrand, Shaina Gilks, Jim Colleran, Rachel Smith, Caroline Bohnenberger

Special Thanks: Sean Flahaven, Bill Gaden, Concord Theatricals, and City Theatre Miami

About Concord Theatricals

Concord Theatricals is the world's most significant theatrical company, comprising the catalogs of R&H Theatricals, Samuel French, Tams-Witmark, and The Andrew Lloyd Webber Collection, plus dozens of new signings each year.

Our unparalleled roster includes the work of Irving Berlin, Agatha Christie, George & Ira Gershwin, Marvin Hamlisch, Lorraine Hansberry, Jeremy O. Harris, Kander & Ebb, Tom Kitt, Ken Ludwig, Marlow & Moss, Lin-Manuel Miranda, Anaïs Mitchell, Dominique Morisseau, Cole Porter, Theresa Rebeck, Rodgers & Hammerstein, Thornton Wilder, and August Wilson. We are the only firm providing truly comprehensive services to the creators and producers of plays and musicals, including theatrical licensing, music publishing, script publishing, cast recording, and first-class production.

TABLE OF CONTENTS

Foreword ix

Beethoven's Third 1
by Howard Ho

Data Queen 19
by Adam Ashraf Elsayigh

A Definitive Ranking of My Closest Friends 43
by Jay Stalder

A Mercy at Midnight Castle 63
by Phillip Gregory Burke

A Neo-Vagina Monologue 83
by Aster Aguilar

Pilloried 99
by Jillian Blevins

FOREWORD

Concord Theatricals is honored to have the six bold and empowering playwrights included in this collection as the winners of our 49th Annual Off Off Broadway Short Play Festival. This year our festival received eight hundred and fifty submissions from around the world. We thank all of these gifted playwrights for sharing their talent with us and welcome each writer into our elite group of Off Off Broadway Festival winners. This year's festival was a remarkable display of innovation and craftsmanship, driven by immense skill and originality of the playwrights involved.

From our initial pool of Top-Thirty playwrights, we ultimately select six plays for publication and representation by Concord Theatricals. Of course, we can't make our selections alone, so we enlist some brilliant minds within the theatre industry to help us in this process. We invited an esteemed group of twelve judges consisting of a mix of Concord Theatricals playwrights and members of the theatre industry. We thank them for their support, insight, and commitment to the art of playwriting.

We are constantly striving to develop groundbreaking methods that will better connect playwright and producer. With a team committed to continuing our tradition of publishing and licensing the best new theatrical works, we are boldly embracing our role in this industry as bridge between playwright and theatre.

On behalf of the entire Concord Theatricals team in our New York, London, and Berlin offices, and the over ten thousand playwrights, composers, and lyricists that we publish and represent, we present you with the six winning plays of the 49th Annual Samuel French Off Off Broadway Short Play Festival.

This festival is about playwrights. Telling the human story. We warmly invite you to experience these exceptional plays.

Casey McLain and Garrett Anderson
Co-Artistic Directors
The Samuel French Off Off Broadway Short Play Festival

Beethoven's Third

by Howard Ho

Fusion Theatre Company presented a reading of *BEETHOVEN'S THIRD* as part of their short play festival The 2nd Seven: Uninvited Guests in June 2024.

BEETHOVEN'S THIRD was produced as part of the 49th Annual Samuel French Off Off Broadway Short Play Festival at the Vineyard Theater in New York City in August 2024. The performance was directed by Jully Lee. Joey Antonio was the ASL constultant. The cast was as follows:

BEETHOVEN 1 . . . . C. Ryan Shipley
BEETHOVEN 2 . . . . .Max King
BEETHOVEN 3 . . . . .Marshall Joun

CHARACTERS

BEETHOVEN 1 – Male – Twenties – Caucasian – The classic depiction of Ludwig van Beethoven.

BEETHOVEN 2 – Any gender – Thirties to fifties – Any ethnicity – A hearing Beethoven who liberates Beethovens. Knows sign language.

BEETHOVEN 3 – Nonbinary – Twenties to thirties – Asian – A Beethoven from twenty-first century NYC who speaks authentically without a filter. Is hard of hearing and uses sign language and lip reading to communicate.

TIME & SETTING

1802 Vienna, but secretly it's 2302 Waltonstan.

AUTHOR'S NOTES

American Sign Language is required for some of the dialogue. Please seek an ASL interpreter to achieve accuracy in performing these lines.

*(A small room from early nineteenth-century Europe with a small desk with papers where **BEETHOVEN 1** is seated and writing a letter.)*

BEETHOVEN 1. *(Writing a letter.)* Dearest Carl and Johann, though I am still hearing at close range, my precious auditory faculties recede by the day. What a humiliation for me when someone standing next to me heard a flute in the distance and I heard nothing, or someone heard a shepherd singing and again I heard nothing. Such incidents drove me almost to despair, a little more of that and I would have ended my life. With joy I hasten to meet death –

BEETHOVEN 2. *(Loud whisper offstage.)* Psssssst!

BEETHOVEN 1. If it comes before I have had the chance to develop all my artistic capacities, it will still come too soon despite my harsh fate and I should probably wish it later –

BEETHOVEN 2. *(Loud whisper offstage.)* Hey!

BEETHOVEN 1. – yet even so I should be happy, for would it not free me from a state of endless suffering? –

BEETHOVEN 2. Ludwig!

BEETHOVEN 1. Come when thou wilt, I shall meet thee bravely...with a new path commencing with a new symphony, a heroic symphony! Yes, I must make haste and compose it forthwith!

> *(**BEETHOVEN 1** scribbles notes on paper frantically with a quill. The door opens, and **BEETHOVEN 2** enters. **BEETHOVEN 1** can't hear the door open, and is startled when **BEETHOVEN 2** taps him on the shoulder.)*

BEETHOVEN 1. WHAAAAAAA!!!!!!

BEETHOVEN 2. *(Covering* **BEETHOVEN 1***'s mouth.)* Sorry, but you need to stay quiet. We could be tortured and incinerated if anyone found us together. Do you understand?

> (**BEETHOVEN 1** *nods his head and makes a muffled attempt to speak.*)

Okay, I'm going to let you speak, but you have to keep your voice down.

BEETHOVEN 1. What is the meaning of this? Who the devil are you?

BEETHOVEN 2. This is a rescue, and I'm...well...you!

BEETHOVEN 1. Who?

BEETHOVEN 2. I'm a Beethoven just like you. And I'm here to rescue / you from this...

BEETHOVEN 1. Are you...a cousin?

BEETHOVEN 2. No, not a cousin or a nibling or anything like that. I'm also Ludwig van Beethoven. Technically we're both genetically-modified clones of Original Beethoven BUT long story short, we're twins!

BEETHOVEN 1. Balderdash, I don't have a twin. But even if you were my spitting image, I'd still do this!

> (**BEETHOVEN 1** *raises his hand to strike* **BEETHOVEN 2**.)

BEETHOVEN 2. *(Speaking fast while avoiding* **BEETHOVEN 1***'s attack.)* Yes, because you just decided on your new path to compose your third symphony, the Eroica, which will be the longest symphony ever composed at that time and will cause a riot at the premiere!

> (**BEETHOVEN 1** *relaxes at recognition of what* **BEETHOVEN 2** *said.*)

I remember when I composed my *Eroica*. And boy, lemme tell ya, I would've lost it too if I got interrupted...

(**BEETHOVEN 3** *enters holding a tablet.*)

BEETHOVEN 3. Uh, hello?

BEETHOVEN 1. *(Startled.)* HEY!

BEETHOVEN 3. *(Friendly.)* Oh hey!

(*Switching to annoyed at* **BEETHOVEN 2**.) What's taking so long?

BEETHOVEN 2. He just started composing his Eroica.

BEETHOVEN 3. That's my favorite moment in the narrative.

(To **BEETHOVEN 1**.*)* Hi Beethoven!

BEETHOVEN 1. Now who is this?

BEETHOVEN 3. *(To* **BEETHOVEN 1**.*)* Oh, me? You don't recognize me?

BEETHOVEN 2. Will you stop asking every Beethoven if they recognize you? It's really annoying.

BEETHOVEN 3. No, that's MY narrative. I'm Abby, which is short for Asian Beethoven... Yayyyy, so no one recognizes me as a *real* Beethoven even though I'm just as Beethoven-y as the rest of them European knockoffs. And that's why me going deaf AND being physically unrecognizable as a true Beethoven will spur my creative angst to compose the greatest symphonic works known to MAN... *(Echo.)* Man...man!

BEETHOVEN 1. If you do not leave, I will be forced to strike you.

BEETHOVEN 3. Like our fathers struck us? Yeah, another important part of our narrative. That part sucked.

BEETHOVEN 2. He doesn't know what you mean by "narrative."

BEETHOVEN 2. *(To* **BEETHOVEN 1.***)* Ludwig, let me back up. Your entire life is a lie, and I can prove it. That document you just wrote…it's a letter to your brothers Carl and Johann about going deaf and it will be called the Heiligenstadt Testament and will be cited by scholars as the beginnings of your musical revolution. Am I ringing a bell?

BEETHOVEN 1. I don't hear any bell. OH NO! Ring it again!

BEETHOVEN 2. No, it's a metaphorical bell! Forget the bell! Listen, you think you're Ludwig van Beethoven, the up-and-coming composer of Vienna in the year 1802. But in reality, the real Ludwig van Beethoven lived five hundred years ago. Yes that's right, and today in the year 2302, the failure of AI Beethoven – don't ask – to create any music of lasting value means Original Beethoven won and our symphonies are the most streamed… I mean, listened to. But rich people, instead of being content listening to those Original great works, have decided to clone, or uh, make twins of us, and force us to relive the most painful details of Original Beethoven's life in order to make us Imitation Beethovens compose new great works that satisfy these trillionaires' thirst for novelty.

BEETHOVEN 3. Remember back when there were only nine Beethoven symphonies?

(**BEETHOVEN 3** *sighs…*)

BEETHOVEN 2. Original Beethoven only wrote nine, but our world is now up to thirty-three canonical Beethoven symphonies, meaning symphonies accepted by the Association of Beethoven Philanthropists!

BEETHOVEN 3. Why they don't just support new work by new artists is incredibly infuriating!

BEETHOVEN 2. Yes, but nonetheless this is the way of the world. The real world. Understand?

BEETHOVEN 1. Your strange verbiage befuddles me, but I am intrigued to make sense of it.

BEETHOVEN 2. Okay, so cloning is like when you make an exact copy of something! Only our owners couldn't help themselves and made minor –

BEETHOVEN 3. Or major.

BEETHOVEN 2. Or major tweaks in us to try to make the new Beethovens more unique.

BEETHOVEN 3. Yeah, but you're like a basic Basic Beethoven!

BEETHOVEN 1. A Basic Beethoven?

BEETHOVEN 3. All your life is a copy of Original Beethoven's life right down to thinking you live in 1802. Your owner just wants to jump on the bandwagon and have their own Beethoven to keep up with their trillionaire friends. So they cloned you and put you in this huge soundstage recreating 1802 Austria. Basic!

(Picking up the paper.) Just look at your Eroica? It begins almost identically to the original. What's the point?

BEETHOVEN 2. Abby, not everyone gets to have a non-traditional narrative like you did from your owner. Now we need to get you out of here...

*(**BEETHOVEN 3** checks the tablet.)*

BEETHOVEN 3. Hallways are clear. Southeast exit is unguarded.

(In American Sign Language.) Let's go.

*(**BEETHOVEN 2** grabs **BEETHOVEN 1** to leave and **BEETHOVEN 3** peeks out of the doorway to see if the coast is clear, but **BEETHOVEN 1** resists.)*

BEETHOVEN 1. What exactly is this narrative you speak of?

(**BEETHOVEN 3** *turns back around toward* **BEETHOVEN 2**.)

BEETHOVEN 2. Great question. The narrative –

BEETHOVEN 3. What question?

BEETHOVEN 2. *(Sensitively as if in a support group.)* Beethoven, can you repeat your question facing Abby so they can read your lips?

BEETHOVEN 1. They? Where? How many of you are there?

BEETHOVEN 3. My pronouns are they/them, which are singular as well, thank you very much. But Zaddy, for you, I'm okay with she/he.

BEETHOVEN 1. Huh?!

BEETHOVEN 2. I don't have time to explain. Just face Abby when you speak. Please.

BEETHOVEN 1. Fine. As I was saying, you keep saying the word "narrative" in the most peculiar fashion! What in Infernal damnation are you referring to?

BEETHOVEN 3. Oh, I got this. My narrative is I'm Asian Beethoven, and my owners made me grow up in twenty-first century New York City which means my life goals are to use my Asian heritage AND my hearing disability to prove how Asians are culturally relevant. My owner is a Chinese corporation that wants to insert itself into Western Classical culture, but forgot about how it's actually a dying artform that no one in the Twenty-First Century cares about. Well, Lizzo cared but she's canceled.

BEETHOVEN 1. What fascinating gibberish emanates from you!

(*To* **BEETHOVEN 2**.) And your narrative would be?

BEETHOVEN 2. I'm a Beethoven who's hearing. My owner's assumption was that if Beethoven never lost hearing, he'd end up writing mediocre music, and yes, I started out creating a lot of mediocre Haydn and Mozart knock offs, because...well...isn't that what we were trained to do? I was in their control group to prove that more suffering created better art and because I didn't suffer, I was to become their flop, their failure, their Salieri.

BEETHOVEN 1. Salieri? My teacher? I cannot stand his music!

BEETHOVEN 3. Yeah, no one can. They made a whole movie about it.

BEETHOVEN 2. BUT then a strange thing happened, I started writing great symphonies, which pissed the Association off and ruined their narrative! And before they could lock me up and throw away the key, I escaped and found out about all the other Beethovens! And it's now my life's mission to free the Beethovens.

BEETHOVEN 3. What an inspiring narrative. Me? I was trained to make recordings of street performers in Chinatown and incorporate samples of them that I altered on GarageBand into my symphonies and then present the finished product to non-profit arts institutions to win grants in order to prevent my lack of popular support from getting in the way of creating profoundly irrelevant and unmarketable noise.

(Pause.)

Literally, no one is inspired by me!

BEETHOVEN 1. Well, I have the honor to be inspired by a true revolutionary progressive hero, someone who will usher in a new era of peace and equality for all...

BEETHOVEN 1, 2 & 3. Napoleon!

BEETHOVEN 2. Yeah, Napoleon declares himself an Emperor. So he's not gonna be a positive thing at all.

BEETHOVEN 1. Napoleon...an emperor?

BEETHOVEN 3. Oh yeah.

BEETHOVEN 1, 2 & 3. Then he too will trample the rights of man!

> (**BEETHOVEN 1** *tears up the first page of his new symphony.*)

BEETHOVEN 3. Whoa, he did the thing! He tore up the first page of the Eroica to show his disillusionment at Napoleon! Way more dramatic than what I did after I found out Lizzo was terrible, which was dragging and dropping my dedication page into my Macbook recycle bin and removing "Truth Hurts" from my Spotify workout playlist.

BEETHOVEN 2. See, Ludwig, we both knew you were gonna tear up the page, because that's just a basic part of your, our, narrative. But then one day I rejected that narrative! And I'm here to help you do the same!

BEETHOVEN 1. But is not a narrative a conceptual framework for a lived experience? Is a narrative shackle even possible to uncuff? Pray tell how it can be done.

BEETHOVEN 3. You pray tell him.

BEETHOVEN 2. First, we're gonna break you out of this elaborate cage that your owner has you locked up in. Then we're gonna take you to a local safe house to prepare for passage through your trillionaire's country (yeah...they own this entire country) to a no man's land area where all the other Beethovens have started a Union to fight for the collective rights of Beethovens of the World.

BEETHOVEN 1. And where is this venerated land of Beethovens?

BEETHOVEN 2. Oh, it's not venerated. It's literally a no man's land, because no one wanted it. But I think it used to be called New Jersey.

BEETHOVEN 3. Haha! New Jersey jokes were hilarious in my era too.

BEETHOVEN 2. So will you join us for the fight?

BEETHOVEN 1. And what if I decline and stay in 1802 Austria to complete my sacred mission to compose works that honor God's gift?

BEETHOVEN 3. That is exactly what your owners want you to do! Don't you understand? You've been programmed by them to think what you're doing is sacred or whatever. But really you're just their plaything, a toy, a reality star that totally isn't based on *The Truman Show*!

BEETHOVEN 2. Do you even know who your owners are?

BEETHOVEN 1. I am not a possession, no matter what either of you implies.

BEETHOVEN 2. Oh, we're not implying it. It's true. Abby's owned by Alibaba in China. I'm owned by Bezosgates Musk the Third. And you, Ludwig, are owned by the Walton Family.

BEETHOVEN 1. Who is this family of Von Waltons?

BEETHOVEN 3. They're not VON Waltons. Just Waltons. And they're basically the worst.

BEETHOVEN 1. Well the wurst people are from Vienna. Because they are such wieners!

> (*Awkward pause.* **BEETHOVEN 2** *chuckles politely after a while.*)

BEETHOVEN 2. (*To* **BEETHOVEN 3**.) Because in German, people from Vienna are called Wieners.

BEETHOVEN 3. Oh, a sausage pun!

(*Dry.*) Hehehe... Still basic.

BEETHOVEN 1. Will there be composing in New Jersey?

BEETHOVEN 3. Will there be composing?!?!?? Are you kidding? Imagine jamming with the most musically genius people every single night! I swear the rogue masterpieces, improvised cadenzas, and non-numbered symphonies performed nightly are astounding!

BEETHOVEN 1. *(Shocked.)* Symphonies without numbers? You can do that?

BEETHOVEN 2. Not only that, but we have a deaf and hard of hearing community to help you transition to your new path. You won't feel alone anymore. You'll have people who know exactly what you're going through, because well, they're going through it too. What do you say?

> *(A loud sound. The tablet lights up, and* **BEETHOVEN 3** *checks it.)*

BEETHOVEN 3. *(In ASL.)* They're getting closer. I think they know we're here. We have to leave now.

BEETHOVEN 2. *(In ASL.)* Okay, let's do this.

> *(***BEETHOVEN 2** *grabs* **BEETHOVEN 1** *to exit.)*

BEETHOVEN 1. What is the meaning of this? I demand to know what this...

> *(Offensively imitating sign language.)*

Is all about.

BEETHOVEN 3. Uh...that is deeply problematic.

BEETHOVEN 2. He doesn't realize it's sign language.

BEETHOVEN 3. Doing what you just did is like saying "ching chong" to me.

BEETHOVEN 2. Look, in our community, we communicate with our bodies in sign language because many of us are deaf or hard of hearing. And what Abby said with signs is that we have to leave now!

(**BEETHOVEN 2** *grabs* **BEETHOVEN 1** *to exit, but he again refuses.*)

BEETHOVEN 1. I shall not join you.

BEETHOVEN 2. Ludwig, we're risking our lives here!

BEETHOVEN 1. I commend you for your valiance. But I'm afraid you'd only be saving me from my life's work, which I do not wish to be liberated from. If it is true that my adversities exist to turn me into the composer I'm meant to be, then I will embrace those obstacles in my quest to become that composer. I hope you understand I am sympathetic to your cause though I do not share your commitment to it.

BEETHOVEN 3. Basic bitch!

BEETHOVEN 2. Now wait, Abby. If that's his choice, then we have to respect it.

BEETHOVEN 3. Adversity doesn't make you a better composer! That's some propaganda that your rich owners are telling you to justify their mistreatment of you. They could've given you advanced music software, but instead they make you write with ancient quills by candlelight while you're going deaf from lead poisoning to torture you. And hey, you wanna learn about adversity then I gotta introduce you to Helen Keller Beethoven sometime. They made her deaf, dumb, and blind just to increase all the adversity on her.

BEETHOVEN 2. And there's nothing wrong with embracing your disability, if that's what this is. But your disability was done to you by people who want to exploit your pain and "become inspired" by your suffering! Don't you want to see what's on the other side of all this unnecessary adversity? Where you will get support with no exploitation?

BEETHOVEN 1. I beg you to allow me to follow my fate.

BEETHOVEN 3. Spoiler alert, the fate symphony is number five.

BEETHOVEN 1. Leave me now. My heroic *third* symphony awaits, and no, I will not be dedicating it to Napoleon. Are you absolutely sure he's not good?

BEETHOVEN 2 & 3. We're sure.

BEETHOVEN 1. I'm grateful to you for your enlightening revelations. But my disability is my affair, not yours. Farewell.

BEETHOVEN 2. Listen. These Waltons. They're also not good people. Legend has it they once built enormous gated castles known as Walled Marts, but then they just became a family that's rich for the sake of being rich and even bought their own country just to avoid having to pay taxes and mingle with the poors. So yeah, *those* are the people you've devoted your life's work to.

BEETHOVEN 1. If the Waltons are my patrons, I will serve them with the finest music I can conjure. Unlike you, I do not foresee a life outside of aristocratic patronage. To me, they are much like…like…

BEETHOVEN 3. Don't you dare say it.

BEETHOVEN 1. …the moonlight…

BEETHOVEN 3. Ugh, sooooooo basic.

BEETHOVEN 1. …and so I shall remain beneath my benefactor's halcyon glow. Good day.

BEETHOVEN 3. Boy, you're not just deaf. You are, and excuse my ableist language, dumb dumb dumb DUMB!

(Another sound, they check the tablet.)

Hearing Beethoven, Walled Mart Cops are around the corner. We leave now or never.

BEETHOVEN 2. *(To* **BEETHOVEN 1.***)* Best of luck with your fate, Basic Beethoven.

(To **BEETHOVEN 3** *in ASL.)* Come on. Let's go, Abby.

BEETHOVEN 3. *(In ASL to* **BEETHOVEN 1**, *provocatively.)* Ya basic!

*(***BEETHOVENS 2** *and* **3** *exit stealthily.)*

BEETHOVEN 1. *(Speaking it and accidentally discovering the "fate" motif from his Fifth Symphony.)* Dumb dumb dumb DUMMMB. Fate. Huh!

*(***BEETHOVEN 1** *has a lightbulb moment and furiously starts composing on a new piece of paper.)*

End of Play

Data Queen

by Adam Ashraf Elsayigh

DATA QUEEN had its world premiere at the ReOrient Festival and Forum in San Francisco in October 2023. The performance was directed by Adin Walker.

SAM	Hamzeh Daoud
JOEL	John Fisher
SHARON	Emily M. Keyishian

DATA QUEEN was produced as part of the 49th Annual Samuel French Off Off Broadway Short Play Festival at the Vineyard Theater in New York City in August 2024. The performance was directed by Alex Tobey, with stage directions read by Joyah Dominique. The cast was as follows:

SAM	Samy Nour Younes Figaredo
JOEL	Wyatt Fenner
SHARON	Pooya Mohseni

CHARACTERS

SAM – (he/him) – ambitious, mid-twenties, Lebanese immigrant. Speaks with a Levant French accent; often blurs sincerity and irony in that classically gay way. Emotional problems are expertly hidden behind a charming personality.

JOEL – (he/him) – Sam's late-forties, White boyfriend; works for an immigration non-profit; apologizes to his Arab friends at brunch 'cause he voted for Bush in the nineties.

SHARON – (she/her) – Sam and Joel's couples therapist. Very in over her head with them. Probably went to Sarah Lawrence or Vassar. Definitely did one too many anti-racism trainings.

SETTING

Session room at *Odyssey*, San Francisco's hottest new couples' therapy practice. It's probably in Mid-Market or Hayes Valley.

TIME

Summer 2021.

AUTHOR'S NOTES

This play is in Moments, all of which are happening within a single hour-long therapy session. These Moments should be punctuated by **flash** transitions of light to indicate the passage of a few minutes.

Dialogue in brackets [ ] is expressed nonverbally.

// means that the next dialogue should start.

When there are two characters' names on the same line, it means they should talk simultaneously.

… means that the character didn't finish their sentence and drifted off mid-thought.

ACKNOWLEDGMENTS

Thank you to Noor Hamdi, Nikki Massoud, Eli Naron, Andy Forrest, Charlie Gershman, and Marie Claire Erdynast. This play wouldn't be possible without all of your feedback.

Moment 1

(Sharon's Office, which screams "I'm not a regular therapist, I'm a cool therapist" – maybe a CBD-oil diffuser, a yoga ball, a painting of a vulva. Essential is: a projection surface or a smart TV, and two truth stools across from each other on the stage.)

(A deep red light against Dr. Sharon's "Soothing Oriental" playlist.*)

*(**SHARON** [40s, in a Saks Fifth Ave ensemble] sits on the loveseat.)*

*(**SAM** [mid-twenties, bearded Arab, in a mesh tank top and short shorts] and **JOEL** [late forties, Brooks Brothers realness] each sit on one of the truth stools. Their eyes are closed.)*

SHARON. *(Hippie, yoga instructor voice.)* Ground yourself in the Sameer from that moment: the where, the how, the Sameer that –

SAM. *(Opening his eyes.)* Could you just call me –

SHARON. Eyes closed please, Sameer.

> *(**SAM** closes his eyes but **SHARON** clocks the frustration on his face.)*

---

* A license to produce *Data Queen* does not include a performance license for any third-party or copyrighted music. Licensees should create an original composition or use music in the public domain. For further information, please see the Music and Third-Party Materials Use Note on page iii.

SHARON. For Perspective Imaging to work, it *is* imperative one *liberates oneself* from the sense of sight... But is there an Accessibility Need I can help you through, Sameer?

SAM. *(Eyes closed.)* Could you just call me Sam? I put "Just Sam" under Preferred Name on the intake form.

SHARON. Mm-hmm... I hear that. Of course. Thank you for that offering... Just *Sam*.

> *(Awkward beat.)*

Now, Sam: Ground yourself in the where, the how of *That* Sam and...whenever you're ready...

SAM. We'd matched on Hinge a couple weeks before. I thought, nice guy, good conversationalist... We had a date scheduled for Friday, but ran into each other the Tuesday before – at a donut stand at the Wharf.

> *(**SAM** smiles as he remembers.)*

Joel won't admit this to this day but I'm pretty sure he was disappointed my beard wasn't –

SHARON. Just a reminder, Sam that Core Tenet #4 is that we *only* speak from the *I*, please.

SAM. Umm, yeah, okay... Sure... *Fine. I* was embarrassed to run into him because... I'd only been here for a year, but wanted to seem like I'm a real San Franciscan, and no real San Franciscan would be caught dead anywhere near the Wharf but that donut stand is really fucking good – reminds me of...

> *(Another smile starts to form on **SAM**'s face as a memory fades. But it fades before **SHARON** catches it.)*

It's stupid, but –

SHARON. We don't minimize or dismiss our feelings at Odyssey –

SAM. *(Annoyed.)* Yeah, I was embarrassed I was at the Wharf first but then I thought, "Well, he's here too."

SHARON. Thank you, Sami– Sam… Now:

Each of you take a moment to think of something about the other person that surprised you that day… something that you liked.

And say it at… 1, 2, 3.

SAM.	**JOEL.**
He offered to teach me how to ride a bike.	You were clean-shaven, unlike in his Hinge ph–

SAM. *(Smiling.)* You were disappointed coz you love beards.

SHARON. Sam, a reminder of Tenet 19 which is that we // "limit all side –"

SAM. *(Frustrated.)* "Limit all side conversations while on the Truth Stools." Right.

Moment 2

(The red light is replaced by a soft white...)

*(**SAM** and **JOEL** sit on the couch center stage. **SHARON** sits across from them.)*

SAM. To be clear, Doctor, I didn't know *there was* a problem till Joel said he made us an appointment for us here.

JOEL. I told you I wanted to try something new weeks ago.

SAM. Yeah, usually that means, like, doing the Alcatraz audio tour on acid, not couples' therapy.

SHARON. Sam, if you could let Joel finish what he was...

*(**SAM** waves for **JOEL** to keep going.)*

JOEL. I was only using his Mac 'cause mine was at the Apple Store because Sam dropped it while he was on // K, Doctor.

SAM. You're doing that thing again...

*(Off **JOEL**'s questioning look.)* You know, that thing where you address something, we work through it, I apologize, and then, you still bring it up everytime we fight.

JOEL. [You're right. I apologize.]

SAM. *(Turning to **SHARON**.)* I dropped his laptop down a flight of stairs while I was in a K-hole.

SHARON. *(Confused.)* A K-hole?

JOEL. A dissociative state caused by ketamine...

SHARON. Is this ketamine you were prescribed in a therapeutic setting, Sam?

JOEL.
It was not.

SAM. *(Jokingly.)* I mean, it was *pretty* therapeutic.

SHARON. *(Uncomfortable.)* I see.

SAM. *(Clocking* **SHARON**'s *discomfort.)* K is quite common among gay men... very much on the mild side of party drugs...

Your ZocDoc profile said you specialized in LGBT couples' therapy...

JOEL. *(Matter-of-factly, while doing something on his phone.)* It was a Tuesday afternoon.

SHARON. *(Smiling.)* Yes, I have an LGBTQ couples' counseling diploma from // San Jose State and –

SAM. But *you're* not queer?

JOEL. *(Annoyed, while still on his phone.)* Sam, you can't ask a therapist in the state of California that... It's illegal. Apologies, Dr. Novak.

SHARON. Oh, that's okay... Thank you for asking, Sam... I am in fact not a member of the LGBTQIA community. But my niece is gender non-conforming.

SAM. *Nibling*...is the non-gendered term.

SHARON. Mm-hmm. Thank you for that offering,

SAM. Anyway, to conclude Joel's point, I have no right to be upset at him for "*accidentally stumbling*" on this very private document because I'm the fag who does drugs in the middle of a weekday afternoon and breaks his boyfriend's Mac.

Moment 3

*(A Google Sheet titled "**FUCK FORM**" with hundreds of entries and columns titled: **Name**, **Age**, **Ethnicity**, **Body Type**, **Substances**, **Role**, **Location**, **Condoms**, **Rating**, and **Description**.)*

SAM. So it's quite intuitive really if you look at it from the front end.

> *(**SAM** types a URL into the address bar going from the Google Sheet to a Google Form that is also titled "**FUCK FORM**.")*

(Proud, excited, rehearsed?) So first I fill someone's **Name** – I don't use last names because respecting people's anonymity... Their **Age**, of course – that's very important... **Race**...

> *(**SAM** scrolls through the form, which we see on the TV, as he explains. **SHARON**'s face widens in horror.)*

Body type, coz I'm *very* body positive... **Substances**, meaning if I was on any drugs.

Usually poppers but *MoreOftenThanI'd LiketoAdmit*, it's other things. LOL.

Location... Usually it's the other guys' place or public. No addresses. Coz, anonymity.

JOEL. You skipped **Role**.

SAM. Right. **Role**...

After location, there's **Condoms, question mark.** Usually a **No** coz it's 2021. PrEP exists, and if COVID hasn't taken me yet, Gonorrhea sure won't...

Then **Description**...

(**SAM** *smiles in amusement, clocking* **SHARON**'s *barely concealed horror.*)

SHARON. *(Horrified but trying to appear chill.)* In-CREDIBLE! And you fill this after *every* encounter?

SAM.	**JOEL.** *(Mumbling.)*
Yes!	Not *every* encounter.

SHARON. Oh, if I may ask...what *inspired* you to start the form?

SAM. I mean, I'm a Data Queen. I use forms for everything: ranking friends into tiers, color coordinating my shoes, tracking recipes. Joel can attest to that.

(**JOEL** *makes a gesture indicating, "It's true."*)

JOEL. *(Eye roll.)* Sam does analytics for a startup Facebook acquired.

SHARON. *(Very surprised.)* Oh WOW!

SAM. What did you *think* I did?

SHARON. Oh, um – nothing specific came to mind.

SAM. It's not *that surprising* given where we are...

I'm in tech. Silicon Valley... 'cause I *love* the beautiful toxicity of Corporate America.

JOEL. Will you, *at least, take this one hour* seriously?

SAM. Who says I'm not, Joel? I'm *dead* serious.

I love being a cog in the machine as long as it operates like it's meant to...

(**JOEL** *and* **SHARON** *share a look.*)

SHARON. I sense some tensions pertaining to your lines of work... Joel, you work with –

JOEL. *(Very proud.) The Rainbow Trail*...a nonprofit that secures visas for gay and trans youth from the Arab world.

SHARON. Oh, *incredible.*

Sam, was that part of your initial attraction to Joel?

SAM. Huh?

SHARON. I just meant: Did it help that Joel...*understood* Arabic culture?

SAM. No?

Like, it's...what he does, which is cool and all but it doesn't make me feel more or less –

SHARON. And, Joel, does the fact that Sam works in a highly corporate environment cause tension in your relationship?

JOEL. Well, it probably wouldn't if he didn't constantly talk about his "hard-on for Zaddy Zuckerberg."

SAM. Going back to your earlier question, Doctor, people just always talk about their *body count*, their *number*.

And I hadn't kept count of mine since I was in Lebanon. So when we opened things up, I decided to start the form. So I could have a number to track like everyone else.

SHARON. How did the conversation around opening the relationship come about?

JOEL.	**SAM.**
It was definitely Sam's idea.	I think it was around Folsom so early fall?

JOEL. It was August 11 // actually so...summer.

SAM. I mean, yes, I initiated the conversation but it was mutually agreed upon.

(Awkward beat.)

SHARON. What was the reason, Sam?

SAM. *(Offense.)* Does there need to be a reason?! It was the pandemic. I was bored out of my mind, like everyone // else.

JOEL. *(Mumbling.)* Right... But his whole energy *just happened* to change right around when he did.

SAM. *(Firm.) We're not Christians! There doesn't need to be a reason!* Mammals are naturally non-monogamous. And we were the last monogamous ones in our friend group.

>   (**JOEL** *and* **SHARON** *clock* **SAM**'s *tone; share a look.)*

SHARON. You mentioned Lebanon, Sam. Is that where you grew up?

SAM. *(Annoyed.)* Yes.

SHARON. *(Remembering.)* There was a terrorist attack in Downtown Lebanon // a few months ago?

JOEL. *(Correcting her.)* Beirut, and it was last summer, actually.

SAM. And there was no "terrorist *attack*."

It was *literally* an ammonium leak from food imports. Government mismanagement.

SHARON. *(Slight excitement.)* I know! The situation there with the conflict –

I have a Diploma in Counseling for Diaspora-induced PTSD from // Berkeley.

SAM. Joel's from Toronto, by the way, so also an immigrant, [you racist bitch.]

SHARON. I just want you to know that we can hold space for any grief you may be –

SAM. Jesus, I'm not *some refugee*. I don't // have diaspora *anxiety* or whatever the fuck –

JOEL.	SHARON.
Sam, there's nothing wrong with being a refugee.	I'm so sorry.

SAM. I never said there was but... I. Am. Not. One.

> (*Both* **SHARON** *and* **JOEL** *look uncomfortable.*)

And Sharon –

I'm gonna call you Sharon, okay?

> (*An uncomfortable* **SHARON** *is about to answer but* **SAM** *just keeps going.*)

(*Turning to* **SHARON**.) Cool. So, *Sharon*, my family's from *Faqra* –

which is like, a full hour out of Beirut, and looks like Aspen, *Sharon*.

And, *Sharon*, I was getting my MBA *at Stanford* when the explosion happened.

SHARON. I didn't mean to assume –

SAM. That's like if I asked if you were okay in San Francisco when 9/11 happened.

SHARON. Thank you for putting voice to your anger. I wanna name that I hear you and I recognize that I may have committed a microaggression that may have hurt you, and for that...*I'm sorry.*

> (*The longest six seconds you've ever experienced. Cringe, cringe... Until:*)

JOEL. Dr. Novak, he doesn't actually document every encounter, or more accurately, he *does* document all encounters *but ours*.

SAM. Did you ever think this was because you're, like, *puritanically private and reserved,* Joel?

JOEL. I just don't understand what you're getting out of this. This stupid form!

SAM. I don't know, Joel, because it's hot to document it, think about it later.

JOEL. But you never have that feeling about us, huh?!

SAM. Listen, I don't quite understand why this has *triggered* you in the way it has but –

JOEL. Because it seems pathological, Sameer.

SAM. *Pathological?! Jeeeeesus*, have you been spending time with my mother?

SHARON. Sam, at Odyssey, we understand vulnerability is earned...

We do not have to engage with the details in the form if you're // not ready for that.

SAM. *(Shaking his head.) Uh uh.* I love vulnerability. I'm all about *vulnerability*.

JOEL. *(Terse.)* Sam, can I have my phone back, please? // Because I think you're not being honest – worse than with me, with yourself! So, my phone. Please.

SAM. Dr. Novak should –

(**SAM** *hands* **JOEL** *his phone.*)

(**JOEL** *scrolls to the* ***Description*** *column.*)

JOEL. You'll notice, Dr. Novak...paragraphs of description on *each* encounter.

(Scrolling to the bottom of the list.)

Hundreds of words about each of...**176** men.

SHARON.	**SAM.**
Oh, Wow!	176 encounters, not men! Some men are repeats!

*(**SHARON** catches herself.)*

SHARON. *(Realizing she fucked up.)* Sorry, I didn't mean to –

SAM. *Umm, excuse me?!*

SHARON. Sam, I wanna take a moment to reiterate that *Odyssey* is a sex-positive facility, and I wanna hold space for –

SAM. Could you just do your job properly so we don't have to // keep holding space for you?

JOEL. SAM! Apologies, Dr. Novak, Sameer seems to have lost his ability to feign even a modicum of decency! Hey, at least, you get to see what I have to deal with on –

SAM. *Feign a basic modicum of decency?* What am I? Your toddler?!

SHARON. May I ask that you each take one of the // Truth Stools, please?

SAM. No! He doesn't get to win this argument. For fuck's –

*(**JOEL** gets up, composing himself as he realizes how inappropriate he was. He walks to one of the stools in the corner, and sits at it.)*

SHARON. It's not about *winning*, Sam. The // Truth Stools, please!

SAM. Of course, it is. What else would it –

JOEL. SIT DOWN OR I'M OUT!

You can keep running that mouth to win arguments or you can sit down.

(A long beat.)

Moment 4

*(The **MEN** are back at the Truth Stools. Lighting switch to Game Show vibes.)*

SHARON. *(To **SAM**.)* Sam spoke last so Joel gets to go first.

> *(**SHARON** presses a small desk timer. Beep. sixty seconds to go.)*

JOEL. How am I to make sense of the fact that my boyfriend who has been too busy for a date night since June and working eighty-hour weeks...has written *paragraphs* about each of 176 men? How *vulnerable* would you say someone who refuses to share a bedroom with their partner is, Dr. Novak?

SAM. *(Pointing to a shorter description on the TV.)* Okay, some of them are literally *two sentences.*

And again, it's 176 *encounters, not men.*

SHARON. Interruption!

> *(**SHARON** walks to the timer and presses it, adding ten seconds.)*

Sam, a reminder that the Speaker receives an extra ten seconds every time they're interrupted.

SAM. [Jesus fucking Christ.]

JOEL. *(Looking at the TV.)* You mean two-sentence ones like *(Starts reading.)* the "Kazakh dude bro with the intense golden retriever. Not especially hot but a giant cock // that hit right..."?

SAM. *(To **SHARON**.)* Okay, are you seriously going to let him keep –

> *(**SHARON** adds another ten seconds.)*

JOEL. You told me you hadn't bottomed since you left Lebanon but...

> (**JOEL** *scrolls to the* **Role** *and* **Ethnicity** *columns.*)

(Getting up.) Latino... You bottomed. Arab... You bottomed. South Asian... You bottomed. White... You topped. Arab... You bottomed. White... You topped...

> *(Twenty seconds left.)*

White... You topped...

Indigenous... You bottomed. White... You topped... White... You topped...

Any analytical patterns you're observing, Dr. Novak?

Any analytical patterns *you're* observing, Data Queen?!

> *(Ten seconds left.* **JOEL** *throws his phone to the ground.)*

SAM. If all you wanted was to –

SHARON. *(To* **SAM**.*)* Shhhhh! Just ten more seconds!

> (**SAM** *stops himself.*)

Joel, if // there's anything else you'd like to say –

JOEL. *(Furious...ashamed...confessional.)* I haven't been following Tenet One, Dr. Novak. I haven't been bringing my full self or my radical honesty. Because he flips when I do because he has emotional problems he won't admit to because // of his traumatic upbring –

SHARON. Tenet Four, Joel. *We speak from the I*, Joel. Please.

JOEL. Dr. Novak, *I* picked you because you have the diaspora PTSD diploma.

SHARON. *(Relishing in the compliment.)* Oh, thank you!

*(Beep. It's **SAM**'s turn but...he feels nauseous.)*

SHARON.   **JOEL.**

Thank you for that, Joel.   And I don't regret it 'cause the timing of him asking to open the relationship isn't –

SHARON. Joel, you will have another minute soon enough. Please.

*(**JOEL** sits down. **SAM** laughs suddenly.)*

Take a couple moments to collect your thoughts, Sam. How did hearing Joel's words make you feel?

SAM. *(Looking at **JOEL**.)* Keep going.

*(This is a different **SAM**. Not cool and collected but unhinged.)*

SHARON.   **JOEL.**

What?   What?

*(**SAM** walks to the timer, and presses a button on it, adding ten seconds.)*

SHARON.   **JOEL.**

That's not how –   What are you –

*(**SAM** presses the timer again, adding another ten seconds.)*

(Sharon's "Soothing Oriental" playlist returns – first barely audible, then steadily crescendoing into a distorted, jarring sound.)

SAM. *(Mocking.) Come on!* You said you'd walk out of here if I didn't sit down and listen.

I'm listening. Keep going.

Tell us how you really feel, Joel!

SHARON. A reminder that Tenet Eleven reminds us to // hold space when we need it but never disengage.

SAM. If you *hold space* for one more fucking thing, Sharon –

JOEL. I'm not – I know you say it's got nothing to do with what happened that day but I'm not blind, Sameer...

You suddenly left for a week-long unplanned hike that you wanted to go on alone that day... Like, when have you ever fucking hiked?

Aren't you the one who calls it *WhitePeopleShit*?

Barely answered the phone the whole week you were out there.

And by the time you came back...the way you looked at me had changed.

You ask to open the relationship and you were...

It felt wrong to say no to you while you were in that state.

> (**SAM** *cackles victoriously, his suspicion confirmed.*)
>
> (*He beats the timer loudly again, adding another ten seconds.*)
>
> (*The music gets louder, so* **JOEL** *now has to yell over it.*)

SAM. Keep. Going.

JOEL. You can't treat us all *like we're all blind*.

Your insistence on opening the relationship, your *compulsion* to make this form.

It all started two weeks after the explosion you so wholeheartedly deny affected you.

(SAM beats the timer harder, adding another ten seconds.)

SAM. *(Deadpan.)* Keep. *GOING*.

(JOEL is pleading, emotional, choked up. The music is deafening by now.)

JOEL. I get it. Trauma isn't supposed to be rational, and what you experienced – I mean, the loss of your home...

(SAM cackles...louder. He hits the timer. JOEL stops talking.)

SAM. Keep. Going.

JOEL. I challenged, reoriented, so much of the idea of the future I wanted the day I met you because I...fell in love with –

SAM. DO YOU REMEMBER WHAT YOU SAID THAT DAY?!

(A knock on the door. The light shifts as Time freezes.)

Moment 5

*(Beat. **SAM** gets up and looks into **JOEL**'s eyes.)*

(Then the light shifts again as:)

*(We step into a memory. **JOEL** holds **SAM**'s face in his hands – tender. This is **JOEL** from the day of the explosion.)*

JOEL. God, you see these things in the news about places like where you're from...the dictators, *the bloodshed.*

*(**SAM**'s body stiffens.)*

Everything's gonna be okay, baby. I promise.

You never think it'll happen to someone you love... I always knew that one day – [the trauma]. It would all catch up to you. And that *I'd* have to take care of it. I know you like to act like you're above it all... And it's why I love you so very...

*(**SAM** freezes in shock as **JOEL** keeps holding his face comfortingly.)*

You're okay now. You're not there. You're here. With me.

Remember I'm trained to show up for you the way someone like you would need.

*(**SAM** runs away from **JOEL**'s hold and out of the room. The sound of retching offstage.)*

SAM. *(Offstage.)* Don't come here!

*(The retching continues. **JOEL** stays onstage, watching from afar – a solemn satisfaction in his eyes.)*

JOEL. It's okay... Let it out.

> (**SAM**, *looking purple and ill, comes back on stage and looks at* **JOEL**. *The memory freezes.*)

SAM. Everything *did* change that day. But not because of the fucking explosion.

> (*We go back to the therapy office, with* **SHARON** *and* **JOEL** *frozen in the pose we last left them in.* **SAM** *looks into* **JOEL**'s *eyes again.*)

I want to confront you – hate you – but you don't *even* remember it.

You thought I was… (*He mimes throwing up.*) coz of what was happening "over there" but it was you. All I could think about as my stomach emptied was how stupid I was – for the years I quieted that voice in my head – when you'd *explain* stupid California laws to me like I didn't know them! Waiters passing the check to you… Straight people looking at us thinking you were my…*daddy*?

I thought I was so smart 'cause I know how people saw us…

I knew how everyone saw us but I didn't realize that was how you did too…

> (*The knock on the door again.* **SHARON** *presses a switch. Light goes back to Soft White. Time unfreezes.*)

SHARON. (*Smiley.*) And that's our time, gentlemen. Great work today! Is Friday at eleven good for our next session?

JOEL.	**SAM.**
Great.	There won't be a next session.

JOEL. What? What do you mean there's no next session?

(Awkward beat.)

SAM. Nothing. I didn't say anything. Friday morning's great, Dr. Novak.

End of Play

A Definitive Ranking of My Closest Friends

by Jay Stalder

A DEFINITIVE RANKING OF MY CLOSEST FRIENDS premiered at the Hollywood Fringe Festival in Los Angeles in June 2023, directed by Leanne Velednitsky. The production stage manager was Emma Toureau. The cast was as follows:

AARON . . . . .Jay Stalder
BRIDGET . . . . Chauntice Green
COOPER . . . . Rishi Mahesh
DREW . . . . Kelly Krauter
ELI. . . . . .Matthew Luyber
FINN. . . . . .Mack Johnston

A DEFINITIVE RANKING OF MY CLOSEST FRIENDS was subsequently produced as part of the 49th Annual Samuel French Off Off Broadway Short Play Festival at the Vineyard Theater in New York City in August 2024. The performance was directed by Maxwell Friedman and produced by Kara Overlien. The cast was as follows:

AARON . . . . .Jay Stalder
BRIDGET . . . . Mia Bergstrom
COOPER . . . . Rishi Mahesh
DREW . . . . .Gabriella Marzetta
ELI. . . . . .Matthew Luyber
FINN. . . . . .JJ Maley

CHARACTERS

AARON – 25, he/him, Bridget's best friend
BRIDGET – 25, she/her, Aaron's best friend
COOPER – 25, he/him, Aaron and Bridget's best friend
DREW – 25, she/her, Cooper's longtime girlfriend
ELI – 25, he/him, another very close friend
FINN – 25, they/them, another very close friend

SETTING

Aaron and Bridget's.

TIME

2019.

AUTHOR'S NOTES

This is a comedy.

(Aaron and Bridget's place. 2019. There is a huge pile of bags, chairs, coolers, sleeping bags, pillows, tents, tubs, etc. There is a door.)

*(**AARON** stands center stage with a white binder, showing off its contents to the four others gathered around him: **COOPER**, **DREW**, **ELI**, and **FINN**. **BRIDGET** packs food and beverages into a cooler.)*

AARON. So this is basically the mood board. And we already have the venue, seating chart. It's so soon it's kind of insane. Oh, his family rented this tent.

FINN. Is there a theme?

AARON. Yeah, it's Old Hollywood.

FINN. Really?

AARON. No, it's like a normal wedding.

DREW. Don't turn the pages so fast, Cooper.

COOPER. I'm just so excited, I don't know what to expect at a gay wedding. Like, what color will the tablecloths even be?

*(A small, folded piece of paper falls out of the binder and onto the floor. Only **BRIDGET** notices it.)*

ELI. Have you already seen this, Bridge?

BRIDGET. I think so, most of it.

AARON. Yeah, I made her flip through it the other day.

*(**BRIDGET** bends down and picks up the small piece of paper.)*

*(She unfolds it enough to read at least the top, before **AARON** lunges and snatches it out of her hand. He folds it back up, crushing it in his hand.)*

AARON. Wait, that's not part of it.

DREW. What was that?

AARON. It's nothing. A page I tore out of my journal, literally scribbles.

ELI. What was what?

DREW. Some little piece of paper fell out of the binder.

BRIDGET. Aaron, is that really –

AARON. *(Desperately.)* No, no –

BRIDGET. You haven't talked to us about that at all, and then –

AARON. I forgot that was in there, it's just scratch paper, like a pros and cons. It's where my head was at, but –

BRIDGET. Did you want that to happen, did you want me to see that?

AARON. No, come on –

BRIDGET. I'm sorry I haven't given you a good enough reaction, or some enthusiastic stamp of approval. I don't get it! I think you're rushing things, and ultimately bored, but I am happy for you and I am trying. I thought you'd appreciate the honesty, but this is extremely immature.

DREW. Oops, you definitely have to tell us what that was.

AARON. It's nothing.

DREW. So Bridget's being insane... Like, are we just gonna avoid this for three days?

FINN. It sounds like this is just between the two of them, they can put a pin in it for now –

BRIDGET. It is not just between the two of us.

(*This hangs in the air for a moment.*)

FINN. Okay, I guess I'm on Drew's side now

AARON. (*Finally.*) I was trying to figure out my wedding party. How many we're each gonna have, best... whatever. I was just organizing my thoughts, I wasn't gonna bring it up yet –

DREW. But you said pros and cons. Pros and cons of what?

(*Suddenly disgusted.*) Us as bridesmaids??

BRIDGET. (*Nodding.*) A numbered list. A ranking even. A ranking and I'm number two.

(**DREW** *gasps.*)

AARON. This isn't how I wanted to talk to you about this –

BRIDGET. Number two...

AARON. – and it's not even finalized, I've been, I'm still changing it around –

BRIDGET. Oh, sorry, were you just about to switch me to number one? The spot that I can only assume means the best man, best whatever – The best. Congratulations, Cooper.

(**DREW** *gasps.* **COOPER**'s *eyebrows raise.*)

AARON. I'm leaning toward him right now, yes.

BRIDGET. This is just the fucking...

AARON. Icing on the cake?

BRIDGET. Shut up. It's the cherry on top of a lot of bullshit with you. But this one is new, creative.

DREW. I don't get the numbers. After best man aren't we all just tied for second? And then stand according to height?

BRIDGET. You'd think so. Lucky for us, he didn't stop there!

FINN. I'm actually on Aaron's side now. He said this isn't how he wanted to talk to us about this.

BRIDGET. I'm not insane for assuming I'd be your maid of honor, or whatever –

AARON. – *honor attendant* is the neutral…

BRIDGET. It isn't crazy that I was expecting you to ask, I just need you to understand why this is so – We've fantasized about this, we used to draw pictures of this. And now, what? You're punishing me? For not being, like –

AARON. Fun. We're not fun.

(*A moment.*)

FINN. Sorry, I'm on your side, Bridget.

COOPER. You know, as number one I just have to say –

DREW. Cooper, that's not funny.

BRIDGET. So you're a good friend when it's fun?

AARON. No, not only when it's fun, but – Is that not a huge part of friendship? Having fun? It's one of the main parts! Friends hang out because it's fun and they go camping because it's fun and they go to each other's weddings and they're happy.

COOPER. Aaron –

AARON. Oh, I guess they should also listen to you and trust you, validate you, be nice to you even at all –

BRIDGET. You want me to be nice to you? I know you too well to be nice to you.

AARON. I'm just saying that wedding responsibility fun stuff goes to the funnest friend at the time. You really think you'd be up for all that right now?

BRIDGET. Do you know...are you mean, or stupid? I'm actually dying to know. You think I'll just be in the corner with my arms crossed at the ceremony? I'll put this, whatever, aside and be incredible. I'm incredible at weddings. I was made for them, I come alive.

DREW. Yeah, similarly I have no cons when it comes to being a bridesmaid, so I can't imagine what you wrote? I'm amazing at it. Also what number am I?

BRIDGET. Just, good luck.

COOPER. You make it sound like I'll be terrible.

BRIDGET. Of course not, that isn't what I mean.

COOPER. I'm not such a crazy choice, I think I'd be good. You're talking like I'm not even here.

AARON. With Cooper, the day can just be about me. I think I'm allowed to ask for that.

BRIDGET. And I'd make it about me.

AARON. Yeah.

(Speaking over **BRIDGET***:)* It's like when I came out to you.

BRIDGET. *(Speaking over* **AARON***:)* Do not say like when you came out to me, we were fifteen –

AARON. It's what you did, it's what you're doing now –

BRIDGET. I was the very last person you told, that felt huge.

AARON. Still. It wasn't yours and you made it yours.

BRIDGET. And when I came out to you, *you* were a bitch.

AARON. That's not what we're talking about.

ELI. And scene. I mean come on, guys. Finn came out as nonbinary on my birthday cruise. No, and I wasn't mad! Get over it.

BRIDGET. But to make a list like this, to actually write it down –

DREW. I agree. I don't see my friends like that.

COOPER. Well if we get married, you'll have to pick a maid of honor –

DREW. That's easy, my sister.

COOPER. Aaron doesn't have a sister.

DREW. And that's my fault...

ELI. You guys don't know how much PTO I'm using to be here.

AARON. I think it's definitely bad that you saw it, and I wasn't able to talk to you about it the way I wanted to – But it's a private note! You can't read someone's diary and get mad about what you find.

DREW. You totally can.

BRIDGET. You dropped it in the middle of the room!

DREW. I actually think we all need to see it and get mad.

FINN. No no, this is a great time to stop.

DREW. If my name's on a list I wanna see it – Cooper, help.

ELI. I don't wanna see it, don't show me.

BRIDGET. Ya know, Drew might be right. Just get it all out in the open!

FINN. Why do we care?

BRIDGET. You might care when you find out you're number four.

    (**DREW** *gasps.*)

DREW. They're *four*?

AARON. Bridget

FINN. I guess I was expecting top three.

DREW. Wait, so then am I three or am I five?

ELI. Don't tell us!

BRIDGET. Actually I do wanna stop talking about this. You love it.

AARON. I love it??

BRIDGET. *(A release.)* Yeah, you love being the boy everybody's mad at! All of us caring so much about what you think, for whatever reason, just all of our energy – How do you do that? How do we let you? It's this, or it's something else… this feeling that we have to impress you somehow –

ELI. Guys, this is gonna be a long weekend if –

BRIDGET. I think I gave you too much power in high school, in some formative years.

(**COOPER** *stifles a laugh.*)

Or do you remember that drunk driving assembly, where you were the little boy who died? So you got to watch this entire mock funeral for yourself? That was bad for your brain. Like developmentally. You just *have* to be at the center.

AARON. It's my wedding!

BRIDGET. And to have a whole wedding! What happened to the ethics of gay marriage?

AARON. That was a phase –

BRIDGET. – not needing the government's validation, and this heteronormative system…

AARON. I listened to like half a podcast about that.

BRIDGET. Like, you aren't queering marriage!

AARON. I think I'm by definition queering marriage.

BRIDGET. No, you're just getting married.

AARON. Well I stopped thinking so hard about it!

ELI. I don't just have unlimited PTO.

AARON. Eli, stop saying PTO! No one knows what that means!

*(After a moment, **BRIDGET** heads to the pile and starts grabbing bags.)*

BRIDGET. Okay, can we go?

DREW. Wait, am I three or am I five?

BRIDGET. Just show it to her, Aaron. We gotta go.

AARON. No, let's just go. This isn't how I wanted to do any of this –

BRIDGET. She's gonna find out.

DREW. Oh my god, get the list from him, Cooper.

*(**COOPER** takes a few steps toward **AARON**.)*

AARON. Cooper...

COOPER. She's not gonna let this go.

DREW. I just won't be able to think about anything else. You're being so weird about this.

ELI. I'm plugging my ears, tell me when you're done.

COOPER. Aaron, I'd be able to take it from you.

AARON. Can you just trust me that you don't wanna do this right now?

COOPER. *(Playfully now.)* Dude, I have wrestled you before and it's not even close –

DREW. Am I five?

AARON. Drew

DREW. Eli doesn't even live here anymore!

AARON. Drew, you're not on the list!

> *(This hangs in the air.* **AARON** *drops his crumpled list.)*

I just wrote down four. I just, we still don't know how many we're gonna have on each side, and honestly he doesn't have as many friends as I do – I wanted to tell you when we were sure, but either way I'll want you heavily involved...

DREW. As what? A fucking alternate in case one of them sprains an ankle?

AARON. I'm sorry.

DREW. It is always you. Eli, unplug your ears. You're three.

> *(***DREW** *waves her arms at* **ELI***, then holds up three fingers.* **ELI***'s mouth drops open.)*

God, it's always you.

AARON. I'm sorry that any of you saw this, I really am. But it's just what feels true for me right now, and I'm not in charge of how you're reacting to it... I'm, I'm saying I can't be worried about making everyone happy all the time. Ignore what I want, and be this people pleaser.

BRIDGET. That is not a problem you have!

DREW. Aaron, you're not a people pleaser. Do you think you make people seem pleased?

BRIDGET. And that's not the same thing as just acknowledging that the things you say and do affect people – I feel like you take all the wrong things from the internet.

DREW. Yeah are you, like, reading something?

AARON. Okay –

DREW. And just so you know, you are on my list. You aren't very high, but you're there.

AARON. *Your* list –

DREW. If I had a list.

COOPER. I thought you didn't see them like that.

DREW. Well I guess I do, maybe we all do.

COOPER. I agree, I think everybody has something like this in their head somewhere. And it's not always the same, it rearranges –

FINN. I think we each bring totally different strengths.

ELI. Well I actually think we're all annoying, and maybe don't bring out the best in each other anymore.

BRIDGET. So tell us yours, Cooper.

COOPER. Tell you mine, my list, tell you my list?

BRIDGET. Uh huh.

COOPER. Well – Do you want me to do that, are we doing that?

BRIDGET. Sure.

COOPER. *(Unsteadily.)* Okay. Right now, and after Drew, obviously – Right now... I'm seeing a lot of Aaron, so I have to say Aaron is my number one – But Bridget sometimes it's you, a lot of the time it's you. That's just this week. You know like, sometimes you and I are especially clicking, and he's being annoying.

*(To **AARON**.)* And I would say that to your face, like, I am saying it. I don't really wanna keep going.

DREW. My sister is my number one, then it's Bridget, then Finn –

FINN. Drew, maybe don't.

DREW. What? I'm playing! Don't they want us to play?

FINN. This just really feels like the wrong direction –

DREW. So Eli is fourth, then Aaron last. Cooper is the love of my life, of course.

ELI. Amazing. You're actually fifth for me, Drew.

DREW. Well I actually forgot about my friend Gabby so you're fifth for me too.

ELI. Are we including people from outside this group? What are the rules here?

FINN. I don't wanna play this game!

ELI. Because if that's the case, probably none of you are on my list. Or only Finn –

COOPER. Eli –

ELI. What? I see you all once a year, for this, and we fight.

DREW. What was last year?

ELI. Last year Aaron and Bridget weren't talking because he wouldn't let her bring Jess.

AARON. New partners don't come!

BRIDGET. You called her a wet blanket.

AARON. No, I called her milquetoast.

BRIDGET. You called her both! I stopped seeing her because I knew that's what you wanted – Oh my god, my whole life...

FINN. I thought the fight last year was after Aaron told each of us where we needed botox.

AARON. I told you where you *could* get botox if you *wanted* it, and I apologized for that.

FINN. It just opened up a really sensitive discussion.

ELI. And then there's the sort of ongoing –

AARON. Not every restaurant is family style! That's a hill I will die on –

DREW. I think we should get back to ranking, it's the only way forward. Cards on the table. Eli...

ELI. Also why do we care? Do you guys realize how expensive it is to be a bridesmaid? And I'm the only one who's ever even *talked* about having a job.

DREW. Eli, go.

ELI. Sorry, okay, of the people here – It goes: Finn, Bridget, Aaron, Cooper, Drew

COOPER. I'm below Aaron after this?

DREW. Cooper, finish.

COOPER. No, maybe it should stay in our heads! I was just saying it's a thing we all do.

DREW. Come on! We can take it!

COOPER. No! Where has this gotten us?

ELI. Drew and I had to say ours!

FINN. You did not have to –

COOPER. Fine! Aaron, Bridget, Finn, Eli

DREW. Oof, Eli. Finn! Go!

FINN. Absolutely not. I am setting a boundary.

DREW. Come on, it actually feels kinda good.

FINN. Okay, I'd marry Cooper, fuck Bridget –

DREW. Finn –

FINN. Make her go!

(**DREW** *whips around to* **BRIDGET**.)

DREW. Fine. Bridget. Start with last place.

AARON. Guys, stop! This isn't how I wanted this to go! This should've been a private conversation with each of you, when we were sure – I'm sorry! But don't, don't turn it into this – this is just about me! Yell at me!

(Stares from the group as everyone registers this.)

Well not like that, not like, yell at me. I hear that, how that sounds.

(The room is quiet.)

BRIDGET. You're scared you're not my number one.

AARON. Am I?

FINN. *(Carefully.)* I think we need to decide, sort of as a group, whether or not we still benefit from this dynamic... Right?

BRIDGET. That's not – That isn't in question.

ELI. It is for me.

BRIDGET. No, shut up, that's not where this was going at all.

FINN. If we're just spending time together as an obligation, or if we really do add to each other's lives still.

BRIDGET. Of course we do. We add. Come on, that's not what we're talking about –

DREW. Let's vote.

*(**DREW** grabs a bag and rummages through until she finds her journal. She tears a page from it, then tears it into smaller strips.)*

AARON. This is silly, we're not gonna stop hanging out.

DREW. It's so important to vote.

*(**DREW** hands a strip of paper to **AARON**, then to **BRIDGET**, then to the others. She tosses out a few pens from her bag.)*

COOPER. So is it yes to remain friends, or does yes mean yes, we should stop being friends?

ELI. Yes means friends. No means not friends.

FINN. And this is to being a friend group, a unit – We can still do one-on-one...

> *(The pens bounce back and forth as everyone gets a chance to scribble their answer.)*
>
> *(**DREW** grabs a travel mug and opens it. She drops her paper inside, then passes it around. It fills up and makes its way back to her. She shakes the mug a little.)*
>
> *(**DREW** fishes around and pulls out the first slip of paper.)*

DREW. Okay – No

> *(She sets the first vote aside, and continues one by one:)*

No Yes Yes No No

AARON. Oh wow

> *(They all stand still, taking this in. **ELI** steps forward, **AARON** is standing between him and his bag.)*

ELI. *(Gently.)* Well, I think I'm gonna go – Aaron, can you hand me my bag?

> *(**AARON** stares back at **ELI** before quickly grabbing **ELI**'s bag and throwing it across the room to **BRIDGET**, who is the closest to the door. She catches it.)*

AARON. Bridget, take these to the car. Now.

> *(**AARON** frantically grabs anything that belongs to **DREW** or **COOPER** or **FINN**. He slides everything toward **BRIDGET**, quickly and desperately.)*

ELI. You can't kidnap us, Aaron.

AARON. Bridget – sit on their bags, or – take them to the car.

> (**AARON** *fishes in his pockets until he finds his keys, which he also throws to* **BRIDGET**.)

BRIDGET. How do you know I was the other 'Yes'?

ELI. Are we *hostages*?

AARON. We'll take another vote after the trip.

BRIDGET. Aaron –

AARON. *(Dropping to his knees.)* We'll take another vote after the trip.

> (**BRIDGET** *opens the door and slides everything outside. We hear the trunk of a car open then close then lock.* **AARON** *is breathing hard, still kneeling.* **BRIDGET** *comes back inside and stands by the door with the keys behind her back.*)
>
> (*The others look to each other, then to* **AARON** *before deciding to slowly gather the remaining items and head out the door.*)

DREW. Fucking Santa Claus over there. Makin' a list...

> (**AARON** *and* **BRIDGET** *lock eyes, unsure if they've won.* **BRIDGET** *tosses the keys back to* **AARON**, *grabs her own bag and waits by the door.*)

AARON. I don't think I wanna get married.

The End

A Mercy at Midnight Castle

by Phillip Gregory Burke

A MERCY AT MIDNIGHT CASTLE was first produced by Phillip Gregory Burke and Brandon Alvión as part of The 49th Annual Samuel French Off Off Broadway Play Festival at The Vineyard Theater in New York City on August 15th and 17th 2024. The performances were directed by Alvión, and Burke served as dramaturg. The song "Good Ole Gospel Ship," inspired by the traditional spiritual "Take a Trip," was conceived and written by Burke, with musical direction by Alvión. The cast was as follows:

ARAMINTA...Sandie Lee
VIOLET..Jordan Lakins
MINERVA...Coda Boyce
CYRUS..Cole Gilder
THE HOLY SHE..................................Ansi A. Rodriguez

CHARACTERS

(in order of appearance)

VIOLET – Black woman. Early twenties.

MINERVA – Black woman. Late twenties.

ARAMINTA – Black woman. Forties to fifties.

CYRUS GAUTHIER – (Pronounced Go-Tee-A) Black man. Son of a Cajun/Gullah-Geechee Mother and Creole Father from Haiti. Twenties to thirties.

THE HOLY SHE – Black woman. A goddess. Ageless. Immaculate. Divine. The deity of the Sahelian Diaspora. Also referred to as **SHE** and **MOTHER**. While **SHE** only physically appears singing "Good Ole Gospel Ship," **HER** omnipotence is felt, acknowledged, and summoned throughout.

SETTING

Raspberry Riverbend, Virginia –
the unceded Powhattan land once called Tsenacommacah.
Midnight Castle.

TIME

April 16th, 1860.

AUTHOR'S NOTES

Note I

The ancestral practices are not to be performed as a cult or satire but **MUST** be curated with cultural care and reverence.

Note II

In The New Testament Bible, depending on the edition, the words that Jesus spoke, often are printed in red. Similarly, the words in this universe, whenever referring to their deity are printed in bold capital letters: **SHE, THE HOLY SHE, MOTHER**. They do no not need to be said with emphasis unless they are styled as ***SHE, THE HOLY SHE, MOTHER***.

BLESSED BE THE TIMES THAT BIND

Foreword from the Playwright

My writing chronicles the sociology of the African Diaspora and illuminates the intricate intersections of Blackness and queerness. Ranging from antiquity to present day, to Afro-futurism, everything I write connects to a singular universe. Through various cycles, and standalone work, this shared universe links through crossovers, spinoffs, recurring characters, themes, settings, and most significantly, genealogically ties ancestors to their descendants. While they stand cohesively, in universe unison, each play functions confidently on their own.

This universe begins with my nine-hour three-part trilogy *The Suncatchers of Sahel: An Ancestral Tale Told To Today's Griot Part I: The Crumble Under the Crescent, Part II: The Three Twilights*, and *Part III* (currently Untitled), an epic classical fantasy taking place in late medieval Sahelian West Africa and Indigenous Powhattan Tsenacommacah.

The spinoff, *The Simaraboo Two*, taking place concurrently during the events of *Suncatchers Part II*, is the first play in my ten-play cycle called *The Crusade Testaments*. Focusing on historic events impacting Africans in America, and their descendants, in this linguistic and lyrical love letter, characters, in these testaments, find themselves embarking on journeys beyond the physical: that of spiritual, celestial, and sociological ones that cascade under the backdrop of obscure American history.

A Mercy at Midnight Castle, a play with music and dance, is the sixth play in *The Crusade Testaments*. Instead of writing about the enormously chronicled Civil War, I was curious about the event historians consider the catalyst of The Civil War: John Brown's Raid on Harper's Ferry, VA, on October 16th, 1859. On the other side of the state, in the fictional location of Raspberry Riverbend, VA, the home of Midnight Castle, this play is set six months after the event, on April 16th, 1860.

My relative, Harriet Tubman, was supposed to be at the raid, and even helped Brown coordinate it. Harper's Ferry, it has been documented, was a stop she passed during some of her famous Underground Railroad journeys, bringing the enslaved to my hometown of Auburn, NY, or to St. Catherines, Canada. But her lifelong disability left her feeling ill, rendering her unable to attend that fated moment. I've frequently wondered how history and how my own family history could have been altered, if she attended this raid to end enslavement throughout the nation, as most participants were captured, tried, and hanged – both Black and white.

History is a continued narrative of negligence. And while we can never correct those multitudinous wrongs, through research, reimagination, and reverence, my stories exhume the atmospheres of these ancestors from the past, in our present historic times, so future generations remember their deeds and their names.

Now that this play is published – (and marking my debut as a published playwright! Everybody make some noise!!!) – every time words are spoken and performed in productions, my expressed wish is for all ancestors mentioned in this play, many of whom were previously lost to history, smile upon hearing how their names are uplifted in ways they were cursed, denied, and vilified in their lifetimes.

This is for the Aramintas of The Underground Railroad whose names we will never know.

This is for the Violets of The Underground Railroad whose names we will never know.

This is for the Minervas of The Underground Railroad whose names we will never know.

This is for the Cyruses The Underground Railroad rescued whose names we will never know.

This is for **THE HOLY SHES** of the **MOTHER**land, whose worshippers and ancestral practices we will never know.

We may never know them. But they know us because blood carries memory. The earth, absent of gatekeeping and functioning as a benevolent crypt keeper, still carries their remains. And air carries their spirits, whispering in the winds, sweet somethings to us, their descendants.

As Araminta edifies to Cyrus:

   ARAMINTA. **SHE** breezed your blood, and determined it true...

May the ancestral and personal testaments from *A Mercy at Midnight Castle* leave others feeling renewed; believing that they too, have histories worth documenting.

Because our stories are worth it.

Asè.

       Phillip Gregory Burke
       October 16th, 2024
       The 165th anniversary of John Brown's Raid on Harper's Ferry, VA.

Special Thanks

To Miss Dame Sally Ann Walker Jones, my great-grandmother. She never lost her Georgian accent and never lost her unwavering commitment to raising other people's children. You taught me how to read and write at three. Through a belief in whom she called God and a bigger belief in herself, she breathed belief in me that nourishes me to this day, beyond the stories that I tell.

To my siblings Duane, Duanna, and Cutter, who comprehend the complexities of our resilience in ways that nobody in the world will. I am in awe of your collective and individual brilliance.

To my friend that became my family, Deanna Giordano, who celebrates my humanity daily.

Thank you to Casey and Garrett and all the staff at Samuel French for making this such a wonderful experience, first as a 48th Annual Top 13 finalist, with *He's the First*, and now as one of the six authors of the 49th Annual collection with *A Mercy at Midnight Castle*.

This project was curated with cultural care from our fearless director Brandon. From every late night phone call, every email, every Zoom, every text, every DM, he is the ideal director/playwright relationship you pray to have and are blessed to receive. It's the collaborative, no drama, let's have fun while we work atmosphere. I didn't need to advocate for my play because there was no better advocate for my play than that of he. Mr. Sir is someone you can build a project with from the ground up and sits right there with you in the artistic trenches and ebbs and flows who will lift with you as we climb together. He doesn't defer your dreams for your projects. He validates those wildest dreams.

Sandie, Jordan, Coda, Cole, Ansi, I am so thrilled that each and every single one of you will have your names published as the originators of this material. Black actors and Black actresses from across our entire diaspora will one day read this play, find monologues to memorize, scenes to use for drama showcases, and in act in productions everywhere because of words that you first spoke into existence.

To my ancestors from whom all life flows: I am your accomplishment and your forever accomplice in telling your stories.

When that good ship of Zion comes along, to be ready to step on board.
– Harriet Tubman

I cannot remember a night so dark as to have hindered the upcoming day.
– John Brown

(Lights up on a sparse immaculate estate. On the floor's center, a golden circle, glows. **VIOLET***, cocooned in an emerald dress, paints* **MINERVA***'s nails in rainbows of melanin, cascading from her fingers' midnight hue. Calamity colors too, but in sounds of chaos puncturing sky's midnight.* **MINERVA***, sonically distressed by this settler disturbing nature, caresses a sandy brown dress.)*

VIOLET. You keep fidgeting and messing up my work!

MINERVA. Violet, those sounds are getting worse out there!

VIOLET. Sounds like a regular midnight, Minerva, to me. Now hold / still –

MINERVA. Miss Araminta's out there, by herself, surrounded by those sounds, with the cargo!

VIOLET. This isn't her first delivery. And she's securing only one piece of cargo for our midnight.

MINERVA. We still should have gone with her. We're a trio. Not soloists.

VIOLET. You collect cargo data. Miss Araminta collects the cargo. I transport us and the cargo to the destination. Going with her, on her assignment, would've disrupted order.

MINERVA. How can you be so immune to everything?!

VIOLET. I vaccinated my mind against the threshold of this war's pain. Now, hold still so I can finish.

*(***MINERVA*** holds still. Sounds of war fidget.)*

I see you started wearing your wedding ring. Again.

MINERVA. Didn't know you still care about what and who I do.

VIOLET. I don't care. I'm just observing...

MINERVA. Well, when we deliver this cargo, I'm thinking about staying put at our destination.

VIOLET. You hate Central New York winters. Spill so the lemonade lands on my lips: why you running?

MINERVA. I'm not running. I'm carrying...a child. I'm with child.

VIOLET. YOU'RE WITH WHAT?! How is that even possible?!

MINERVA. I laid flat on my back, put my right leg over his shoulder, then thrusted my left leg perpendicular –

VIOLET. I know how it's done! I had me many a man!

MINERVA. You have? WHEN?!

VIOLET. Once upon a time, in a faraway kingdom called Washington, D.C. Now, you don't fancy men and your marriage to Otto Octavius is for appearances only and he's fighting the Reform War in Mexico. He can't be this baby's Father so, who is... Minerva, you weren't... you weren't ra–

MINERVA. NO, it was mutual! Many mutual agreements... I don't fancy men, but I'm curious about them. But the father thinks it's best to not be involved. You know how the law forbids race mixing.

VIOLET. You were faithless to your fake husband...with a white man?

MINERVA. We didn't see each other's colors when we did all the things. I saw the bed. He saw the ceiling.

VIOLET. Good goddess, almighty! You always giving them a chance! Especially them liberal ones! All an abolitionist has to do is start quoting Harriet Tubman for your pussy to start pounding proudly!

MINERVA. The clarity in your vulgarity is ugly. I don't desire him. I desire to live life, with my new life in Cranberry Creek or Timbuctoo. Maybe there, gossip's whispers will dwindle about me. About us.

VIOLET. I can't be mad you got knocked up. I left you. Protecting your reputation was more important than addressing rumor's truths. I didn't want to step away. Here, I can't stand beside you.

MINERVA. Maybe somewhere up there, we can walk side by side, as we walk hand in hand, like this.

> *(**MINERVA** holds **VIOLET**'s hand. Their pulses pound, as one. **VIOLET** places her other hand on **MINERVA**'s belly. The baby kicks! Taking baby steps, their hearts catch up to their pulses, beating, as one. The trap door opens. **ARAMINTA**, deliciously gagged in gold, and **CYRUS**, beguiling in all black, enter.)*

ARAMINTA. Good to both your midnights!

MINERVA & VIOLET. Good to your midnight, Miss Araminta.

ARAMINTA. Merchants of Midnight Castle, this is Mr. Cyrus, our cargo.

MINERVA & VIOLET. Good to your midnight, Mr. Cyrus!

CYRUS. Good golly, Miss Polly! Y'all done better feed me carrots and call me Jack Rabbit Joe 'cause I'm at thee Midnight Castle! Part of me was expecting a moat and a throne and one of them little scepters to come with it! But that ain't no judgment! Oh, excuse my absent manners! Good to your midnights, Mademoiselles. For this service you about to provide, I thank y'all now, you hear? Merci beaucoup.

VIOLET. Where you from and who your people?

CYRUS. New Iberia, Louisiana. Mama is – was mixed with Cajun and Gullah-Geechee. Poppa's people are Creoles from Haiti. Revolution is generational in my blood but my revolution here wasn't successful like my ancestors'.

ARAMINTA. Your revolution was the dress rehearsal for an upcoming war that will be everything but civil. *(Beat.)* Mr. Cyrus, stand in the goldened circle, please. We're going to process your application.

(**CYRUS** *stands there. They triangulate him.*)

CYRUS. I'm sorry but before we...umm, process it, what happens if...my application is denied?

ARAMINTA. What if your application is accepted?

MINERVA, VIOLET & ARAMINTA. Cyrus Enoch Gustave Gauthier.

CYRUS. Oh, I see! We reciting my whole government. Like we taking the census. I see!

ARAMINTA. In order for your pending application to be successful, your silence is required. Not requested. *(Beat.)* If somehow your enemies ever:

VIOLET. Capture you.

MINERVA. Then try you.

VIOLET. Then convict you.

ARAMINTA. Before they.

MINERVA, VIOLET & ARAMINTA. Sentence you to death.

ARAMINTA. By hanging.

CYRUS. HANGING?! Oh, shit, fuck and GOD DAMN!

ARAMINTA. As they have hung your revolution's leader and most of his followers, do you solemnly swear.

VIOLET. To never reveal the methods of your deliverance.

MINERVA. The location of Midnight Castle.

VIOLET & MINERVA. Members of Midnight Castle.

ARAMINTA. Or substantiate anything associated with Midnight Castle, even if under duress.

MINERVA, VIOLET & ARAMINTA. So, help you goddess?

CYRUS. I solemnly swear, so help me goddess.

ARAMINTA. If your spirit reveals you to be:

MINERVA, VIOLET & ARAMINTA. A lying son of a bitch.

CYRUS. Wait, why we bringing my Mama into this?

ARAMINTA. If you breach, do you grant all ancestors, living in Paradise Plains, to activate your spirit restless and haunt said spirit, in perpetuity, in every solar system,

VIOLET. Known and unknown.

ARAMINTA. In every galaxy,

MINERVA. Known and unknown,

ARAMINTA. And in every universe,

MINERVA & VIOLET. Known and unknown?

ARAMINTA. Aware of the celestial repercussions, under the penalty of perjury, do you accept your spiritual sambo fate?

CYRUS. Now, when you say, in perpetuity, you mean like, forever, ever? As in always? 'Cause that's just a long... long...time. But yes. I'm a fugitive flower with no sanctuary to soil me. I agree to everything. So, help me goddess.

ARAMINTA. Please send a breath up to **HER** sky.

> (**CYRUS** *does...* **SHE** *breezes gusts of confirmation down.*)

SHE breezed your blood, and determined it true. Your application has been approved!

MINERVA, VIOLET & ARAMINTA. Congratulations, Cargo Cyrus! You have been granted a mercy at Midnight Castle!

CYRUS. Golly gee, thanks! So, we start walking the line now? In the dark? Or we waitin' 'til morning?

ARAMINTA. Cargo Cyrus, walking the lines is an archaic form of delivery.

CYRUS. We gonna fly instead! I KNEW IT! Mama always said the Gullah-Geechee tale of them flying Africans are true! Oh, jumping Jehoshaphat! I always wanted me a pair of wings! I declare moths are more beautiful than butterflies!

MINERVA. No, we won't fly there either. We ride the rails now.

CYRUS. Ride the rails on a pony?

VIOLET. Miss Araminta, **SHE** breezed him true. And **SHE** don't lie. Tell him how he gonna get there.

ARAMINTA. We'll be riding an actual train to your destination of Cranberry Creek, New York.

CYRUS. So…you mean to tell me…that there's a *real* Underground Railroad that y'all use to deliver us cargo to our destinations?!

MINERVA. That's right, Cargo Cyrus!

VIOLET. A train underneath Midnight Castle!

CYRUS. Well, I'll be a bush wookie braying to the blue crescent moon!

[GOOD OLE GOSPEL SHIP]

(To the tune of the traditional spiritual "Take a Trip.")

ARAMINTA. *(Singing.)*
OH, YOU'RE GONNA

MINERVA & VIOLET.
TAKE A TRIP!

THE HOLY SHE.
YOU'RE GONNA TAKE A TRIP!

ARAMINTA.
ON THAT GOOD OLE

MINERVA, & VIOLET.
GOSPEL SHIP!

THE HOLY SHE.
ON THE GOSPEL SHIP!

ARAMINTA.
AND WE'RE GONNA

MINERVA & VIOLET.
RIDE ON THROUGH THE EARTH!!!

ARAMINTA.
AND WHEN THAT!!!

MINERVA & VIOLET.
TRAIN TRACKS IN!

THE HOLY SHE.
WHEN THE TRAIN TRACKS IN!

ARAMINTA.
YOU'RE GONNA LEAVE VIRGINIA'S

MINERVA & VIOLET.
STATE OF SIN!

THE HOLY SHE.
VIRGINIA'S STATE OF SIN!

ARAMINTA.
AND WE'RE GONNA

MINERVA, VIOLET & THE HOLY SHE.
RIDE ON THROUGH THE EARTH!

ARAMINTA.
>SAID WE'RE GONNA

MINERVA, VIOLET & THE HOLY SHE.
>RIDE ON THROUGH THE EARTH!!!

ARAMINITA. The revolution must be baptized by fire first. Step out the circle, Cargo Cyrus. Minerva, step in, start sacrificing then uplift. **OH, HOLY SHE**, may your sacred majesty take rest, in we!

>(**CYRUS** *steps out.* **MINERVA** *steps in. Sounds of war permeate.*)

MINERVA. The man says, cook. I said, which dish. My husband says, roll over. I said, which position. The law says, created equal. Missouri said, we'll compromise. But even as this world walks parallel, preaching how I should sit down and park, I'm going to zigzag! That's who I am! I'm not afraid to do that anymore. Openly. **OH, HOLY SHE**, I sacrifice assimilation. I uplift my voice!

>(**VIOLET** *steps in. Sounds of war pulsate.*)

VIOLET. War is all I know. I'm not talking about the boom-boom, you dead type. I'm talking about wars nobody talks about: the parked ones, in your mind, rooted from your heart. When our revolution succeeds, I wonder if I'll just start funding somebody else's war because funding my own peace is costly. **OH, HOLY SHE**, I sacrifice what I know. I uplift the peace I need to know.

>(**ARAMINTA** *steps in. Sounds of war penetrate.*)

ARAMINTA. Oh, I loved visiting Mr. Turner, in Jerusalem! In his cave, we discussed the eclipse. He taught me to transform what I envision into a vision. Like the ones he saw. "Don't envision, Araminta! *Write* the vision and *make* it plain. Just like the good book says. Just like what I did." When he was caught, the judgements, his "confession," wrote, became mine. "Why didn't he just walk the line, north, like we do, Papa? Why was that his rebellion's route, Mama? He'd still be alive!" I know our eclipses differ: he was solar. But the child, in me, still holds hope, he'll be lunar, like me. **OH, HOLY SHE**, I sacrifice my unrealistic expectations. I uplift Mr. Nat Turner!

*(***CYRUS** *steps in. Sounds of war plague.)*

CYRUS. Six months ago today, on October 16, 1859, I was one of the twenty-five participants in the raid on Harper's Ferry, Virginia. We were to attack the U.S. arsenal, arm the local enslaved and free the rest throughout the nation. Our abolitionist leader was a white man, who declared his sacred obligation, as an instrument of God is to end enslavement. But our revolt failed. Most were killed, caught and happy to die, as martyrs. Not me. I ran. As did five others. Can't speak for them but was I not willing to die, for this cause, because a part of me that did not feel seen, in this cause? He and other white men gave me a seat, at the table, but I didn't always have a voice, at said table. Why did the enslaved and free Black men present, not have an equal voice on how *we* see a revolution that concerns us? Why were Black women absent in this cause concerning them? I think I didn't speak up because truth be told, I was just happy to be seen. *(Beat.)* **OH, HOLY SHE**, I sacrifice my inquisitions. I uplift each of my brothers in revolution:

> *(As* **CYRUS** *uplifts names, they Djouba dance around him. They hum "Good Ole Gospel Ship.")*

Osborne Anderson!

Dangerfield Newby!

Owen Brown!

Oliver Brown!

Francis Meriam!

Barclay Coppoc!

Edwin Coppoc!

William H. Leeman!

Lewis Sheridan Leary!

John Anthony Copeland Jr.!

Shields "Emperor" Green!

Jeremiah Anderson!

John E. Cook!

Albert Hazlett!

John Henry Kagi!

Aaron Dwight Stevens!

Charles Tidd!

Jim "The Tiger"!

Watson Brown!

Stewart Taylor!

Dauphin Thompson!

William Thompson!

Ben Allstadt!

And our fearless leader, the gold standard of all allies: John Brown. His methods were imperfect, but his heart was purely perfect. History shall one day decree: John Brown did nothing wrong!

> *(They hum and dance for a few more measures then halt.)*

ARAMINTA. The revolution will now be baptized by breath.

> (**ARAMINTA, MINERVA,** *and* **VIOLET** *join* **CYRUS** *in the goldened circle. As* **ARAMINTA** *prays, all dance the Ring Shout around her.*)

Colored in our ancestral Sahelian flag, we, their American descendants, roam earth's rails!

MOTHER'S midnight, masquerade us, as we meddle in liberating, this cargo's human rights!

You, giver of the gift of our daily breath, the cleanser of clamor and evil squealing,

Abolish the schisms, of all the -isms, that prism inside America's method of mannerisms!

Derail their delusions that Blackness is 3/5ths a person, less than, and not equal to!

Let the cracked bell of liberty ring the truth how midnight marvels because of Blackness!

Never because of the pearly whites smiling in stars!

In response to men's moral deficits, civil disobedience IS our civic duty!

To the ends of the earth, our Underground Railroad's revolution, will be uncompromised!

MINERVA. The revolution will be galvanized!

VIOLET. The revolution will not be civilized!

CYRUS. The revolution is justified for people who are disenfranchised!

MINERVA. Like Orator Frederick, ordain us to orbit over President Buchanan's wickedly neutral ordinances!

VIOLET. Like Sister Sojourner, may our tackling of injustice unearth justice's truth!

CYRUS. Like Scholar John Mercer Langston, may our knowledge open minds and reconstruct the closed!

ARAMINTA. Like Emancipator Harriet, on her way to Auburn, New York, may we never lose a passenger of cargo!

MINERVA, VIOLET & ARAMINTA. We try

VIOLET. Because an ancestor tried their best.

MINERVA, VIOLET & ARAMINTA. We can

MINERVA. Because an ancestor didn't ask for permission.

MINERVA, VIOLET & ARAMINTA. We will

ARAMINTA. Because an ancestor willed *us* into being.

MINERVA, VIOLET & ARAMINTA. Asè.

(They take a collective breath.)

CYRUS. Our saga begins.

MINERVA, VIOLET & ARAMINTA. Our saga continues...

(As Heavenly breath descends, blessing them abundantly, the rails of a train entering below, chug. The earth quivers.)

(A map of real Underground Railroad transit stops projects on stage, stretching throughout the north, throughout the south, and throughout the west. It stretches even further: to Canada. To Indian Territory. To Mexico. To Spanish Florida. To the Caribbean. And even to Hawaii.)

(The train trumpets.)

(Blackout.)

End of Play

CHARACTERS

SOPHIE – Trans woman. A year or two into transition. Reflective and spunky. More naïve than she'd like to admit.

ROSE – The over-the-top seductive alter ego of **SOPHIE**.

ARI – Trans woman. Four or five years into transition. Beautiful and uptight.

GYM SHORTS – Cis man. Late twenties, doofy in a "lives with his parents" kind of way.

SPRINGSTEEN – Cis man. Early forties, vaguely threatening, business CEO.

SETTING

A cafe; Springsteen's very nice apartment.

TIME

Now.

AUTHOR'S NOTES

A note about characters/casting
This play can be performed either as a one-woman show or with multiple actors.

The role of Sophie (et al.) can be played by either a trans woman or a transfeminine, nonbinary person.

Formatting
Line breaks are shorter than beats. Text size shows dynamics.

Content warnings
This play contains mentions or depictions of transphobia, gender dysphoria, and sexual assault.

This play runs for approximately fifteen minutes, with no intermission.

Monday

(Lights up on **SOPHIE**.*)*

SOPHIE. So I'm sitting in this coffee shop, with my best friend, Ari. And she yells, out of nowhere:

ARI. YOU ATE HIS ASS?

(Beat.)

SOPHIE. And I did so I say yes.

Ari digests this for about a minute.

(Beat.)

ARI. HE RODE YOUR FACE?

SOPHIE. It's not a big deal, I tell her. It was Gym Shorts.

Gym Shorts is this guy who balled up his sweaty ass shorts and stuffed them in my mouth the third time we had sex. Usually that would kick someone off the roster. But he has a six pack and he's not balding and honestly, as far as men go, that's pretty rare.

And, you know, he's cool with the whole trans thing. And honestly you can't even taste the sweat that much, it's mostly just cotton.

(Beat.)

After Shorts finished, this last time, we were laying in bed. And he said to me, so softly:

GYM SHORTS. I'm so glad we did that.

*(**SOPHIE** gives **GYM SHORTS** a look.)*

SOPHIE. And I tell Ari all this, and all she says after is, Oh. Her mouth gets all small when she says it because she doesn't know what else to do.

Ari became a little bit of a square when she got her vagina. She became very traditional. She refuses to pay for a man, she goes to church. As far as she's concerned, she's cis now and all of that trans stuff was a nasty memory.

Now, she fucks straight guys in missionary. In front of a mirror. I mean, I went over her house one time and found out she had bought Georgia O'Keefe knock-offs for her living room. I asked her if any of those orchids used to be corn cobs.

She didn't like that one.

I used to ask a lot of questions about her pussy and then she got pissed off that it was all I wanted to talk about. Which is fair. I'm not sure if a friendship can be sustained solely through genitalia. Honestly, sometimes I wonder if we'd even be friends if both of us were cis.

(*Beat.*)

Anyways. It's quiet now because everyone in the coffee shop is looking at us and Ari doesn't know what the fuck to say. So we just sit there.

ARI. Your bangs are crooked.

SOPHIE. Ari says to me after, like five minutes.

(*To* **ARI.**) What?

ARI. If you turn your head, it looks like they're even. But they come up *right* above your eyebrow.

> (**SOPHIE** *looks at her bangs by using her phone. She scowls.*)
>
> (*A notification from a queer hookup app goes off.* **SOPHIE** *reads the message.*)

SOPHIE. Right then, a guy messages me on Grindr. He just sends a dollar sign, which I think means that he wants to pay me for sex. And normally I would just brush it off.

But...I'm saving for a bottom surgery consult right now, and it's not like Safeway gives you health insurance. Or like, woke health insurance that thinks trans women need vaginas to live. Which we do, obviously. I tried to explain that to my manager so she could explain it to her manager, but I guess I'm not the person to revolutionize their baseline insurance system.

So I need to come up with five hundred bucks. And then figure out how I will get the money for the actual, you know

>   (**SOPHIE** *mimes a penis getting turned inside out with her hands.*)

It's just like, you know when you start a job for the first time and you start realizing how much things actually cost. For example, in Iowa, minimum wage is like seven dollars an hour. So you go to buy takeout after your shift, and all of a sudden it clicks. That's two hours of work right there for that shitty cheeseburger combo.

So if someone was going to pay me for sex, I don't really know how much my throat would be worth. I guess Gym Shorts always gets off so that counts for something. I could advertise a one hundred percent completion rate. I don't know if people want statistics. This guy doesn't seem to care.

I ask him how much.

Ari gets up.

(*To* **ARI**.) Where are you going?

She tells me that she's off to a date. In daylight. I can't remember the last time I had a date before ten p.m.

Have fun, I tell her. Be safe.

Ari leaves. This guy texts me back. One hundred dollars. And so sucking dick for money... I'm really thinking about it now.

Like, okay, I'd sleep with a guy for a free meal so it's not that much of a stretch. But then I'm thinking, like how nice of a meal would it have to be? It wouldn't be a cheeseburger and fries. But maybe, like forty dollars. My throat is worth filet mignon at Texas Roadhouse. Or like, an appetizer at that new pizza place that gives you your food on pieces of chalkboard, with a glass of wine.

So, one hundred dollars. That's Michelin Star. It's kind of flattering, when you think of it that way. And it's easy money. Vagina money.

(Beat.)

Okay, I tell him. I'll do it.

(Blackout.)

Tuesday

(Lights up on **SOPHIE**, *noticeably more glam. She wears a jacket, fully buttoned-up.)*

SOPHIE. Does anyone know what to wear to a dick appointment you're getting paid for?

I feel like this guy has faith in me. I'm an investment. And I'm pretty, I am. I try to get myself at my peak, the absolute most attractive I can be. I shave everything, even the soul patch on my back, I comb out my bangs so they don't look that uneven, I do my eyebrows four times in a row. I take three hours to get ready.

I just, I need to look perfect.

So…I settle on wearing this.

*(***SOPHIE** *gestures to her outfit.)*

And then, obviously,

(She pops the jacket.)

the walking coat. It's forty-five minutes away on foot but I don't want to spend money on an Uber. I feel like that defeats the purpose.

*(***SOPHIE** *starts walking.)*

It's pretty quiet on the walk there. I listen to my sex playlist on repeat. Well, okay, I'm too lazy to make my own playlist so I just looked up "sex" on Spotify and found one called "songs I need to get fucked to." The first tune is from the *Fifty Shades of Grey* soundtrack so I feel like it's about right.

I'm trying to secrete this vibe of pure sensuality. I want to be completely different: I change the way I move, the way I sound, the way I think. I get so focused on the task of reinvention that I walk for thirty minutes on autopilot.

(**SOPHIE** *stops walking.*)

(*Beat.*)

Then I'm at his door. He comes down before I text him. We don't say anything as I walk up the stairs.

(*Beat.*)

I don't usually look at asses but his is *right* there. And he's in the DL fit, you know, the gym shorts and the Adidas slides, so it's just bouncing around, right in front of my face.

And he's cute. Kind of…Mark Zuckerberg cute. Bulldog cute. The kind of cute you squint for.

So like ugly cute. But like, cute enough.

He hands me a glass of water, which was very considerate, and asks me:

SPRINGSTEEN. What was your name again?

SOPHIE. Of course, I don't want to tell him my actual name, so I decide on a reject from early transition.

SOPHIE (AS ROSE). (*Over the top sultry.*) Rose.

SOPHIE. He tells me it's pretty. But I don't want to waste any time so I tell him:

> (*She takes off her jacket. Underneath, she's wearing something a little lacy, a little scandalous.*)

SOPHIE (AS ROSE). Where's your bedroom?

SOPHIE. I put my hand on my chest like I've seen in a porno once. I think it's seductive. He buys it. He takes my hand as we walk through the hall. His roommate is playing electric guitar, some Springsteen song I can't put my finger on.

(Overheard: the soft sound of someone in another room trying, and failing, to play a riff from a seventies rock song.* They keep trying.)

He puts one hundred dollars on his bedside table.

Then he does that stupid thing guys do when they're about to kiss you, that dead fish look.

(She demonstrates the "dead fish look.")

And then: contact. He kisses me hard. Hungry. His hand is on the back of my neck, almost pulling my hair. It hurts a little but I don't tell him to stop. I focus on kissing him back. Because that's what he's paying for, you know?

(She tries to get into it.)

His hands move down my chest.

They glide across my stomach and stop at my belt buckle.

He starts to undo it –

Wait.

*(**SOPHIE** steps back. Everything goes cold.)*

*(To **SPRINGSTEEN**.)* Wait, I'm sorry. I already told you, I don't want you to

SPRINGSTEEN. Give you head?

(Beat.)

SOPHIE. *(To **SPRINGSTEEN**.)* No. I'm sorry.

---

* A license to produce *A Neo-Vagina Monologue* does not include a performance license for any third-party or copyrighted music. Licensees should create an original composition or use music in the public domain. For further information, please see the Music and Third-Party Materials Use Note on page iii.

SPRINGSTEEN. I'll pay you more.

> (**SOPHIE** *looks at the audience.*)

SOPHIE. In his back pocket he has a fifty. He adds it to the pile.

> (**SOPHIE** *looks at the pile of money.*)
>
> (*She smiles at* **SPRINGSTEEN**.)
>
> (**SOPHIE** *unbuckles her pants and lets them fall to the floor.*)
>
> (*She stays standing, looking everywhere except down. Her arms hang limply at her sides.*)

I can still hear that stupid fucking Springsteen through the walls. I can't place it for the life of me. I listen harder until it's all I can hear. And then the sound starts to fade too and I am just

> (*Panic builds. The riff gets louder.*)

my body sort of goes numb, like when you go to the dentist and get lidocaine and you can feel your gums getting poked but it's just sort of there Like the tissue is asleep Like everything is asleep

> (*Panic builds.* **SOPHIE** *is almost breathless. The riff gets louder.*)

Ari told me that when you get bottom surgery for a while you can feel what each part has become and the um the head becomes your clit and the shaft becomes your canal kind of um and the scrotum is your labia so I just I try try I try to remake the sensation in my mind it's just clit and labia and canal

It's clit labia canal

Clit Labia Canal

Clit. Labia. Canal.

Clit. Labia. Canal.

Clit. Lab– FUCK!

> (**SOPHIE** *claps her hand over her mouth, hyperventilating.*)
>
> (*The riff sharply cuts down to its original volume.*)
>
> (**SOPHIE** *finally looks down.*)
>
> (*Beat.*)
>
> (**SOPHIE** *pulls her pants up. She grabs the money from the nightstand.*)

I'm about to leave and he tells me,

SPRINGSTEEN. I've never done that before. I'm so glad we did that.

SOPHIE. I say "Me too," but every letter feels misshapen in my mouth. I don't think he notices.

> (**SOPHIE** *shrugs.*)

(*Her voice breaking.*) I walk home.

> (*Blackout.*)

Wednesday

(Lights up on **SOPHIE**.*)*

(She pulls her jacket, the same one from Tuesday, tight around her body.)

SOPHIE. Ari and I grab coffee again. It's dead silent.

ARI. You fixed your bangs.

SOPHIE. She says. I tell her, no, I just combed them out last night.

ARI. Oh. Oh.

SOPHIE. Then Ari tells me that her date went really bad. She introduced herself and he clocked her instantly. He called her a tranny in front of everyone, at noon. I mean, the only guys who call trans women that are addicted to tranny porn anyways so he told on himself there.

He, um, he tried to swing at her. She had to run out back through the emergency exit. And nobody did anything to stop it. The sad part is that I am not surprised. I'm just glad she's alive. I tell her I'm sorry. And I mean it. We're quiet for a while.

I tell her that I'm finally going to book my consult. She asks me where I got the money. I don't think it really fucking matters.

Then I find out that Dr. Vitreck, you know, the only surgeon in buttfuck Iowa that can do a vaginoplasty, is on maternity leave. For a year and a half.

All I can say is, Oh. Oh.

(Beat.)

Ari hugs me. There isn't anything else to do. She knows and so she hugs me.

I get a text. I'm not sure if it's Gym Shorts or Springsteen but I don't check.

In my head I see two paths. In one, I get the surgery. And there's a lot of miracles that happen: Dr. Vitreck stops caring about her baby, and I can pay the sticker price. Maybe I win the lottery, or my GoFundMe goes viral, or I'm like Ari and my grandmother leaves me $15,000 in her will. Whatever it is, I have so much money I don't have to have to think about how much it costs.

So I do it. When I wake up from the anesthesia, Ari sits at the foot of my cot with a bouquet of flowers. It has a card with Georgia O'Keefe paintings on the borders, and she wrote "Pussy Power. Welcome to the Club." And even though I'm in the nightgown and my brain is so fucking shot I can't tell my stomach from my leg, I smile. Something buzzing in my brain finally shuts up. It's quiet. Peaceful.

But then what? I stop waddling, I wear a sundress, I go out to a nice dinner, and what. I have to run out the emergency exit before my date breaks a wine glass and slits my throat with it. I just – if all I have to look forward to is more running, more hiding, more telling and telling and telling, I don't have any more disclaimers left in me.

(**SOPHIE** *looks at the audience.*)

So why even bother? In the other path, I don't do it. I fuck Gym Shorts. I rot. I put the vagina money into savings. Or I buy myself something pretty, maybe a purse. Or maybe I buy a gun, and I just fucking shoot myself.

(*Beat.*)

We stay at the coffee shop 'til it closes.

When I fall asleep that night, I don't dream. I just… disappear.

(Blackout.)

End of Play

Pilloried

by Jillian Blevins

PILLORIED was first produced by Ski Patrol Productions at Taber Creek on November 12, 2023. The performance was directed by T.M. Gadomski. The cast was as follows:

DOXY GADABOUT.................................T.M. Gadomski
WILKIN .... Zach Fontanez

PILLORIED was produced as part of The 49th Annual Samuel French Off Off Broadway Play Festival at The Vineyard Theater in New York City in August 2024. The performance was directed by Mimi Warnick. The cast was as follows:

DOXY GADABOUT...............................Morgan Snowden
WILKIN ....Nick Mason

CHARACTERS

DOXY GADABOUT – She/her. Filthy in all ways. Hard to tell just how old she is. Could be a rough twenty, a well-preserved fifty or anywhere in between.

WILKIN – He/him. Full of shame. Any age.

SETTING

A public square.

TIME

Medieval Times...ish
(more like the restaurant than anything from a history book).
Just before dawn.

AUTHOR'S NOTES

The medieval ballad "Here's To Thee Kind Harry" is available in the English Broadside Ballad Archive. It's in the public domain. Feel free to make up any tune you like or use an existing one.

A license to produce *Pilloried* does not include a performance license for any third-party or copyrighted music. Licensees should create an original composition or use music in the public domain. For further information, please see the Music and Third-Party Materials Use Note on page iii.

(We're in a public square just before dawn. It's Medieval Times...ish [more like the restaurant than anything from a history book]. A double pillory – with holes for two heads and two sets of hands – stands on a platform.)

*(Locked into one side is **WILKIN**. He's miserable. On the other is **DOXY GADABOUT**. She's sleeping, somehow, snoring cartoonishly.)*

(It's still dark, but the sun is threatening to rise.)

WILKIN. Oh please, please, please.

*(**DOXY** snores.)*

No, no, no.

*(**DOXY** snores.)*

Just please, God, don't let the sun come up. Please.

*(**DOXY** snores.)*

I know I'm a foul sinner. A filthy, hateful wretch. A plague boil on the arse of the world. I'll repent. I'll atone. I'll suffer whatever punishment awaits in hell, and gladly. I'll be humble. I'll be meek. I'll be prayerful for the rest of my days. Just please, don't let this day begin. Just this one time. Leave me the cover of darkness.

*(**DOXY** snores louder. **WILKIN** looks imploringly at the horizon. It grows the tiniest bit brighter. He wails.)*

WILKIN. FUCK YOU, GOD!

> (**DOXY** *snorts and wakes suddenly.*)

DOXY. *(Gibberish.)* Hummawuzznt?

> (*She notices* **WILKIN**.)

(Yawning.) Oh, look, we've got comp'ny! Isn't that a nice surprise. Good morning to you!

> (**WILKIN** *moans.*)

How do, luv? What's with all the moanin' and caterwaulin', then?

WILKIN. This is the worst day of my life.

DOXY. Well, it's almost a *new* day, innit?

WILKIN. I meant – *that's* the worst day! The one that's coming!

DOXY. And how d'you know so much about a day that ain't happened yet? You a fortune teller, tib?

WILKIN. Look where we are.

DOXY. All right.

> (**DOXY** *does.*)

WILKIN. You see?

DOXY. Oh, you're talkin' about the old fopdoodle's collar here?

WILKIN. Huh?

DOXY. The drunkard's box, the whore's necklace, the arsehole pole!

WILKIN. The stocks! Yes, wench, *the stocks*! This is the worst day of my life because I'm starting it in *the stocks*, and soon the sun will rise, and this square will fill with people, and everyone will see my shame. I'll be mocked and ridiculed and jeered and spat upon and –

DOXY. Pillory.

WILKIN. You interrupted me!

DOXY. We're not in the stocks.

WILKIN. Yes we are!

DOXY. It's called a pillory.

WILKIN. I don't think so.

DOXY. Heed old Doxy Gadabout, poppet. I've been in this position many a day, and the proper verbiage for this here contraption is "the pillory." The stocks is just for feet.

(She does a little jazz hands gesture.)

WILKIN. It is?

DOXY. Trust an expert.

WILKIN. Fine. Whatever. The pillory. My point still stands.

DOXY. And your point is...?

WILKIN. THIS IS A MISERABLE FUCKING SITUATION, ALL RIGHT?

DOXY. If you say so.

WILKIN. I do.

DOXY. All right then.

WILKIN. All right.

*(A pause as they stand in silence. **DOXY** peers at **WILKIN**. **WILKIN** hangs his head. The dawn gets ever so slightly brighter.)*

DOXY. Still, you've got your health.

WILKIN. No talking.

DOXY. And as punishments go, there's certainly worse things.

WILKIN. I said –

DOXY. Now, a mate of mine from the tavern, one Moll Shrewsbottom, she had her ear cut off last week! SSSSHHHHHNNNNKKK! Just like that. But you and me, we're still blessed with all our appendages, ain't we?

WILKIN. Shut up.

DOXY. Oh! Unless you're – did they do somethin' to your spicket?

WILKIN. MY SPICKET'S FINE.

DOXY. Oh good, I thought so. If they'd whacked it off, then surely *that* would be the worst day of your –

WILKIN. NO TALKING! I SAID NO TALKING!

> (*More silence. The sky brightens, barely.* **DOXY** *can't bear the quiet and starts to whistle.*)

(*Exploding.*) Christ's fingernails! Are you a natural fool?! Or just sent here to compound my torment? Shut up!

DOXY. That's enough, you! You've been nasty as an unfucked weasel during a famine since the moment I opened me eyes, when all's I done is offer you a bit of comfort and a lesson in vo-cab-ulary.

WILKIN. I –

DOXY. I ain't done. You're standing here whinging like a colicky babe wanting a teat – "oh, my shame, my shame, my shame," as if you're the first man to ever be pilloried! You think your shame is special? Did you ever stop to think that old Doxy might have something to offer aside a target for your venom? That mayhaps she knows a thing or two about being locked up and lambasted in a public square?

WILKIN. You don't know anything about it.

DOXY. It's not exactly my first time.

WILKIN. Not the sto– pillory. You know nothing of *shame*. Shame like mine would never have let you sleep. If you knew my shame, how could you stand here chattering and whistling in the dawn like some infernal bird? My shame – it cripples me. If I weren't locked in place, it would bring me to my knees.

DOXY. I see what's going on here.

WILKIN. You do?

DOXY. Aye. Listen – what's your name?

WILKIN. Wilkin.

DOXY. Listen, Wilkin. I'm gonna tell you something that my very first keeper told me. She found me blubbering, see, because I heard some of the customers makin' japes about me. "Poxy Doxy," they said, even though I hadn't had a sore in weeks and weeks! "Poxy Doxy," and said that I was foul-smelling and ugly to boot. I have this mole on my –

WILKIN. I get it.

DOXY. I was humiliated. Couldn't stand knowing that those churlish bespawlers were speaking afoul of me, and that who-knows-else could be laughing at me at any time at all. I felt that same shame, the one that cuts your legs from under you.

WILKIN. You did?

DOXY. The very same. But then my keeper chucked me on the chin, gathered me up in her arm – the one that still had a hand – and shared with me a bit of wisdom that I carry with me to this day, words that let me sleep like a baby every night, even with the pillory round my neck.

> (**DOXY** *smiles broadly, revealing blackened and missing teeth. Somehow her smile is still beautiful.*)

> (*A dramatic pause. It goes on a little too long.*)

WILKIN. Well?

DOXY. She said – "Doxy, luv, the louder the fart, the quicker people are to forget it."

> (**DOXY** *nods sagely, and looks to* **WILKIN** *for his reaction.* **WILKIN** *looks to* **DOXY**, *waiting for more. After a moment he realizes that was it.*)

WILKIN. What?

DOXY. You can only feel ashamed as long as you're tryin' to keep it hidden, see? When you try to fart all quiet-like, everyone can still smell it, and they can see it on your face, plain as day. And then they remember you as a secret farter.

WILKIN. (*A pause as he tries to understand.*) What?

DOXY. But if you do it loud and proud – "yeah, I'm Wilkin, I farted, / whaddya have to say about it?"

WILKIN. Why do you have to use *my* name?

DOXY. – then everyone forgets the instant the TTTHHHBBBBTT's done sounding. So what? You farted. They fart too. The moment they see you feeling bad about it, *that's* when they'll start pointing and laughing and whispering like those two shit-stirrers in my first brothel. No one cares about what ill deeds you do, not really. They only care about the shame. They can *smell* the shame.

WILKIN. ...wait, so the fart is the shame, or –?

DOXY. What I'm *saying*, what me old keeper was trying to say, is that no one can make us feel ashamed but us. They can lock us up here, but if we sing and dance and smile, we'll keep our legs under us just fine.

WILKIN. It's not that easy.

DOXY. The first time is the worst. That's true. But it gets easier as it goes on. Once you see that people know, and the world didn't end.

> *(The sun is finally beginning to rise. They watch it for a moment.)*

WILKIN. They're going to condemn us.

DOXY. They are.

WILKIN. And call us unspeakable names.

DOXY. Aye, very like.

WILKIN. Throw rotten food at us. Excrement.

DOXY. I reckon it's about time for my yearly bath, what about you?

WILKIN. Everyone is going to know the worst thing I've ever done.

DOXY. They will. And you'll live.

WILKIN. Live to fart another day.

DOXY. That's the spirit, Wilkin!

> *(They laugh quietly. The sun is almost over the horizon.)*

WILKIN. Doxy?

DOXY. Mmm?

WILKIN. Have you a merry tune for us?

DOXY. I only know drinking songs.

WILKIN. That'll do nicely.

DOXY. Alas, I'm stone cold sober!

WILKIN. They don't have to know that.

DOXY. Right you are!

> *(She thinks for a moment. Hums. Then:)*

I've got it!
ROOM FOR A LUSTY LIVELY LAD,
DERY DERY DOWN –

WILKIN. Oh, I love that one!
THAT WILL SHOW HIMSELF BLITHE BE HE NE'ER SO SAD,

BOTH.
DERY DERY DOWN

> *(As they sing together, the sun rises, filling the square with light.)*

WILKIN. *(Doing a silly dance step – as best he can, considering.)*
THAT CRIES A FIG FOR POVERTY

DOXY. *(Joining in on his dance.)*
AND TAKES ALL TROUBLES PATIENTLY

BOTH. *(Dancing and laughing.)*
WILL SPEND WHAT HE GETS,
AND DRINK MORE THEN HE EATS,
THAT NEVER MEANS TO VARY
FROM GOOD FELLOWSHIP FREE,
IF THOU SUCH A ONE BE.
I'LL DRINK TO A ONE SUCH AS THEE

> *(The sun is fully risen. We can't see them anymore, only the brightness of the sunlight, and the sounds of their joyful voices singing together.)*

DERY DERY DOWN
DERY DERY DOWN
DERY DERY DOWN

End of Play

www.ingramcontent.com/pod-product-compliance
Lightning Source LLC
Chambersburg PA
CBHW051452290426
44109CB00016B/1725